KD 4080 SPE

D1644655

DE
AP)

DATE DUE FOR RETURN

CANCELLED ACCESSION

The Options for Britain and Northern Ireland

Sarah Spencer and Ian Bynoe

INSTITUTE FOR PUBLIC POLICY RESEARCH

30–32 Southampton Street, London WC2E 7RA
Tel: 0171 470 6100 Fax: 0171 470 6111
E-mail: ippr@easynet.co.uk
Web site: http://www.ippr.org.uk
Registered Charity No.800065

The Institute for Public Policy Research is an independent charity whose purpose is to contribute to public understanding of social, economic and political questions through research, discussion and publication. It was established in 1988 by leading figures in the academic, business and trade-union communities to provide an alternative to the free market think tanks.

IPPR's research agenda reflects the challenges facing Britain and Europe. Current programmes cover the areas of economic and industrial policy, Europe, governmental reform, human rights, defence, social policy, the environment and media issues.

Besides its programme of research and publication, IPPR also provides a forum for political and trade union leaders, academic experts and those from business, finance, government and the media, to meet and discuss issues of common concern.

Trustees

Lord Eatwell (Chairman)
Gail Rebuck (Secretary)
Robert Gavron (Treasurer)
Professor Tony Atkinson
Kumar Bhattacharyya
Rodney Bickerstaffe
Lord Brooke
James Cornford

John Edmonds
Professor Anthony Giddens
Lord Hollick
Philip Hughes
Sir Jeremy Isaacs
Professor David Marquand
Jan Royall

(MILE END)
QMW LIBRARY

Production & design by **EMPHASIS**
ISBN 1 86030 060 X
© IPPR 1998

Contents

Acknowledgments

IPPR has received considerable assistance from many individuals and organisations in preparing this report and would like to thank them for the time they have given to share their ideas and to comment on our draft proposals. They bear no responsibility for the conclusions we have reached.

In particular we would like to thank Chris Sidoti, the Australian Human Rights Commissioner; Brian Burdekin, Special Advisor to the UN High Commissioner on Human Rights; Pamela Jefferies, Chief Commissioner of the New Zealand Human Rights Commission; Barney Pityana, Chair of the South African Human Rights Commission and John Hucker, Director General of the Canadian Human Rights Commission for the time they gave us to talk through the experience of their Commissions. We are similarly grateful for the time given to us by the heads of UK public bodies and their colleagues: Joan Smyth, Chair and Chief Executive of the Equal Opportunities Commission (Northern Ireland) and Evelyn Collins, its Principal Equality Officer; Sir Bob Cooper, Chairman of the Fair Employment Commission; Michael Lavery QC, Chairman of Northern Ireland's Standing Advisory Commission on Human Rights, and Denise Magill, its Research Officer; Elizabeth France, Data Protection Registrar, and Francis Aldhouse, Deputy Registrar; Sir Herman Ouseley, Chairman of the Commission for Racial Equality (GB) and Barbara Cohen, its Legal Officer; Kamlesh Bahl, Chairwoman of the Equal Opportunities Commission (GB) and Frank Spencer, its Policy Director; Sir William Reid, then Parliamentary Commissioner for Administration for England and Wales; William Bingley, Chief Executive of the Mental Health Act Commission for England and Wales, and to the officials with whom we were able to discuss aspects of our proposals in the Home Office, Northern Ireland Office, FCO and DfEE. Our thanks also go to Lord Lester QC for his advice and support; to Norman Warner, Senior Policy Advisor to the Home Secretary; John Cridland (CBI); Elizabeth Melling (ORC) Julie Mellor and Ian Clyde.

We would like to thank Rowena Daw for giving generously of her time to contribute her expert knowledge and her editing skills; to Michael Head, for his paper estimating the cost of the Commission; to Marie Pool for her substantial first draft of the chapter on national human rights institutions abroad and Beth Ginsberg for additional research on that chapter. Our thanks to Françoise Hampson for chairing the Consultative Conference in December 1996 which contributed much to our thinking on this issue and to the Shadow Home Secretary Jack Straw MP, as he then was, for addressing that conference; to the 1990 Trust for the joint seminar which enabled us to consult black organisations and the TUC for similarly enabling us to hear the views of union representatives; and our colleagues in Liberty (the National Council for Civil Liberties), the Scottish Human Rights Centre, the Committee on the Administration of Justice in Belfast, Charter 88, the Constitution Unit, Justice and the School of Law at Kings College London, for their varied contributions and support.

We thank the Danish Centre for Human Rights for enabling us to participate in the Second Meeting of European National Institutions on Human Rights in Copenhagen in February 1997; and all the contributors to our conference on Commonwealth Human Rights Commissions which we organised jointly with the Commonwealth Human Rights Initiative on 16-17 October 1997 and which assisted us to see the issue of a UK Commission within its global context.

Finally, our thanks to all of the organisations and individuals who responded, by meeting us or in writing, to our Consultation Paper on the options in December 1996 and our subsequent paper in May 1997, a list of whom is attached as Appendix 4.

IPPR would like to acknowledge its considerable thanks to the Nuffield Foundation for funding both the research for this report and the Consultative Conference in December 1996.

The views expressed in this report are those of the authors and not necessarily those of the IPPR, its staff or Trustees.

About the authors

Sarah Spencer is the Director of the Human Rights Programme at the Institute for Public Policy Research and a former General Secretary of the National Council for Civil Liberties (1985-9). She established the Human Rights Programme in 1995 with support from the Joseph Rowntree Charitable Trust and has edited or co-authored IPPR reports on immigration, Citizenship, policing, constitutional reform, a Bill of Rights and the rights of children and young people.

Ian Bynoe was, at the time of writing, a part time IPPR Research Fellow specialising in social and human rights. A solicitor who has worked in law centres and in private practice, he was Legal Director of MIND from 1990-1994. He was the co-author of *Equal Rights for Disabled People* (IPPR 1991) and has also written *Beyond the Citizen's Charter* (IPPR 1996) and *Rights to Fair Treatment* (IPPR 1997). He also provides legal and practice training to local authorities and NHS Trusts on disability, health and social services law. He was appointed a member of the Police Complaints Authority in August 1998.

A Human Rights Commission for Britain and Northern Ireland?

Home Office Minister, Lord Williams of Mostyn QC:

'We are not ruling out the idea of a human rights commission. We believe that we should have the best possible material available before we decide, first, whether to have one and, secondly, what its terms of reference and proper parameters should be.'

'...it is very important that we get the nuts and bolts and practicalities right after taking evidence and approaching the matter with care. The constitution and nature of the human rights commission, if there is to be one, is very important. It is extremely important that we get it right first time.'

House of Lords debate on the Human Rights Bill , 24 November 1997

Labour Peer Baroness Amos, former chief executive of the EOC:

'We currently lack any systematic monitoring, enforcement or promotion of human rights in the United Kingdom. We have bodies such as the EOC and the CRE which have some responsibility for the protection of certain human rights, but their coverage is partial. We need a body which will raise public awareness, promote good practice, scrutinise legislation, monitor policy developments and their impact, provide independent advice to Parliament and advise those who feel that their rights have been infringed. I am particularly keen to see the promotion of an inclusive human rights culture which builds on the diversity of British society. That would be a key role for any human rights body to play.'

House of Lords debate on the Human Rights Bill , 24 November 1997

Retired Law Lord, Lord Simon of Glaisdale:

'I repeat that informed opinion is now overwhelmingly in favour of a human rights commission. A parliamentary committee, admirable though it may be, is no substitute.'

House of Lords debate on the Human Rights Bill , 24 November 1997

Lord Irvine of Lairg QC, the Lord Chancellor:

'Well, the Government certainly hasn't ruled it out forever, the Government has ruled it out for the present. Incorporation of the Convention is going to operate as a very substantial culture change. We want it to percolate into the workings of all the courts, we want a human rights culture to develop throughout society. And what we intend to do is to stand back and watch this bed down and monitor the success, or otherwise, of the system that we have introduced and if it appears to us after that bedding down period that it would be better also to have it underpinned by a Human Rights Commission, then no doubt that is something that we'll turn our attention to.'

Radio 4 Analysis, 6 November 1997.

Paul Murphy, Minister of State, Northern Ireland Office:

'When the (Northern Ireland) Commission is formed, we will have one of the strongest human rights institutions in Europe...It will be a powerful voice and force in developing, through education and research, an active human rights culture in Northern Ireland'.

House of Commons debate on the Northern Ireland Bill, 27 July 1998.

1. Introduction

On 24 October 1997 the Government published its Human Rights Bill to incorporate the European Convention on Human Rights into the UK's domestic law. It was a historic landmark, coming 46 years after the UK ratified the Convention in 1951 and 31 years after people in the UK were first allowed to petition the European Commission and Court of Human Rights if they believed that their rights under the Convention had been infringed.

Incorporation will, in the Government's words, 'bring human rights home'. It will allow individuals to argue for their Convention rights in the UK's own courts and tribunals without taking the long and expensive road to Strasbourg. The Bill was the beginning, Lord Scarman said, of a new constitutional chapter in our history.[1]

The changes which the Government has said it hopes will result from this legislation: that individuals will be able to access their Convention rights in court; that legislation will be scrutinised more carefully to avoid any infringement of the Convention; that public authorities will ensure that their actions do not infringe rights; and that a culture of rights will develop, are indeed the developments which are needed. The object of this report, however, is to question whether those objectives are attainable in the absence of a public body charged with ensuring that the legislation is effective: a Human Rights Commission which could take the necessary steps to ensure that the changes which the Government has itself identified as necessary, do occur.

A Human Rights Commission is a statutory body established to protect and promote human rights. Internationally there are a growing number of such bodies, known as national human rights institutions, with varying functions, structure and titles. In Commonwealth countries they tend to be known as Human Rights Commissions. This report sets out the case for a Human Rights Commission in the UK and examines the options for that body and for the Commission which is now to be established in Northern Ireland: their potential roles, functions and structure; their relationship with existing organisations and with Government and Parliament, and what the UK Commission might cost.

The movement to establish such bodies has been strongly endorsed by the United Nations. The General Assembly in 1993 approved a set of principles on which national human rights institutions should be based, the *Paris Principles* (see Appendix 1). In the same year the

Vienna Declaration from the World Conference on Human Rights agreed to encourage the establishment and strengthening of these bodies, 'recognising that it is the right of each State to chose the framework which is best suited to its particular needs at the national level'.[2]

The Council of Europe is also keen to promote the establishment of such bodies in each of its Member States. In its most recent Recommendation on this issue it suggested that the role of such bodies should include:

> drawing the public authorities' attention to, and advising them on, human rights matters and promoting the provision of human rights information and education to the public.

It urged Member States to consider establishing a Human Rights Commission and to ensure that the terms of the Resolution were 'distributed in civil society, in particular among non-governmental organisations'.[3]

The British Government is aware of the important role which Human Rights Commissions play in other countries and endorses their development. It has provided assistance to a number of Commissions abroad, contributing funds for exchange visits, training and office equipment.[4]

The Government has recently agreed to establish a Human Rights Commission in Northern Ireland and has given serious thought to whether it should establish such a body in Britain. In a pre-election Consultation Paper on incorporation, *Bringing Rights Home*, in December 1996, Labour had noted that, after the passage of the Act incorporating the ECHR, it would be important to:

- provide advice and guidance for those who wish to assert their rights

- institute or support individual or public interest cases based upon well-researched, well founded evidence and arguments

- conduct inquiries into particular issues or legal areas

- monitor the operation of the Act

- scrutinise new legislation, and

- ensure the conformity of EU law with human rights obligations under international treaties.

One way forward, the paper had said, would be for the Act to establish a Human Rights Commission or Commissioner to take on some or all of the roles described, possibly in stages. It noted, however, that this would require careful consideration of the implications for existing public bodies in the field - the Equal Opportunities Commissions in Great Britain and in Northern Ireland, the Commissions for Racial Equality, the National Disability Council and the Fair Employment Commission.

In a separate proposal, the paper suggested that Parliament should establish a Joint Committee on Human Rights to monitor the operation of the new Act 'and other aspects of the UK's human rights obligations'. It should have the powers of a Select Committee to compel witnesses to attend. If draft legislation was identified as having an impact on human rights, it could be subject to scrutiny by the committee.[5]

Labour's manifesto for the May 1997 general election contained a commitment to incorporate the European Convention but included no reference to establishing a Human Rights Commission. Nevertheless, shortly before the election, Labour agreed with the Liberal Democrats, in the Report of their Joint Consultative Committee on Constitutional Reform, that a Commission should be established:

> A Human Rights Commissioner or Commission, or similar public body, would provide advice and assistance to those seeking the protection of the rights enshrined in the Convention, and be itself able to bring proceedings to secure effective compliance with the ECHR, whether by judicial review or by representative proceedings on behalf of a number of people.[6]

Non-governmental initiatives

Meanwhile, two non-governmental organisations, the Constitution Unit and the Institute for Public Policy Research, had each begun to think through the potential roles and structure of the proposed body. Prior to these initiatives, the need for a Commission had been identified by bodies such as the National Council for Civil Liberties (Liberty) but little attention had yet been paid to the detailed form which the Commission might take.

Some of the many Private Members Bills which had been introduced since the 1970s to incorporate the European Convention had made provision for a Commission, including a Bill sponsored by Liberal Democrat Peer, Lord Lester. The Human Rights (No 3) Bill sponsored by Graham Allen MP in 1993 provided for a Human Rights Commission whose members would be drawn from the legal profession, NGOs and the public, with powers to monitor the Act; initiate proceedings in its own name; conduct formal investigations; issue codes of practice; examine all Bills to ensure conformity with the ECHR; undertake educational activities and give financial assistance to organisations concerned with promoting human rights.

In the Autumn of 1996, the Constitution Unit gave the first detailed attention to these issues in its report on incorporation of the ECHR, *Human Rights Legislation*. It considered whether a new Commission was necessary rather than merely desirable, in particular if Parliament were itself to establish a Human Rights Committee to monitor compliance with the ECHR and other human rights instruments.

It concluded that without a Commission the impact of incorporating the ECHR was likely to be diluted and that a Commission could play a key role in nurturing a culture of rights and responsibilities and in promoting the effective enforcement of the guarantees provided by the ECHR and effective access to the courts.

The Constitution Unit argued, moreover, that incorporation of the ECHR could make victims of violations *worse off* if resources were not made available to improve access to justice; and that one way to do that would be through a Human Rights Commission. Incorporation would, it noted, require complainants to take their case through the domestic courts before the European Court of Human Rights in Strasbourg could consider their case and this would amount to an additional hurdle if inadequate financial support were available to enable them to do so.

Finally, the Constitution Unit argued that many of the important functions of a Commission - the provision of information to the public, and research, as well as the provision of financial assistance for taking cases - could not be fulfilled by a Parliamentary Committee, however necessary in its own right.[7]

IPPR began its own research in September 1996 and issued an options paper for a Consultative Conference in December of that year. The Conference was addressed by many of the heads of existing public bodies whose responsibilities include promoting aspects of human rights (see Appendix 5) and the Consultation Paper led to official responses from most of those bodies (Appendix 4). Our ideas were influenced by the responses we received and a subsequent paper was circulated to interested organisations, and to the incoming Government in May 1997. IPPR then contributed to the debate which preceded publication of the White Paper and Human Rights Bill in October. Completion of this report was postponed in order to take into account the extensive debates on the Human Rights Commission issue during the passage of the Human Rights Bill through Parliament, and the subsequent Commons debates on the establishment of a Human Rights Commission in Northern Ireland.

White Paper *Rights Brought Home*

Shortly after the election, Lord Irvine had told a public audience that a Human Rights Commission could be a 'driving force for change' but indicated that the Government might nevertheless defer the decision on whether to establish such a body because of cost considerations and concern over its potential impact on the existing equality Commissions. This was indeed the outcome with no provision being made for any kind of statutory body within the Human Rights Bill.

The accompanying White Paper, *Rights Brought Home: The Human Rights Bill*, said however that the Government:

> has not closed its mind to the idea of a new Human Rights Commission at some stage in the future in the light of practical experience of the working of the new legislation.

It did not consider that the new body was central to achieving the Bill's objectives and noted that:

> Some reservations have been expressed, particularly from the point of view of the impact on existing bodies concerned with particular aspects of human rights, such as the Commission for Racial Equality and the Equal Opportunities Commission,

whose primary concern is to protect the rights for which they were established...

The Government's conclusion is that, before a Human Rights Commission could be established by legislation, more consideration needs to be given to how it would work in relation to such bodies, and to the new arrangements to be established for Parliamentary and Government scrutiny of human rights issues. This is necessary not only for the purpose of framing the legislation but also to justify the additional public expenditure needed to establish and run a new Commission. A range of organisational issues need more detailed consideration before the legislative and financial case for a new Commission is made and there needs to be a greater degree of consensus on an appropriate model among existing human rights bodies.

The White Paper repeated the suggestion that Parliament might establish a Committee on Human Rights and proposed that one of its main tasks might be to conduct an inquiry:

into whether a Human Rights Commission is needed and how it should operate. The Government would want to give full weight to the Committee's report in considering whether to create a statutory Human Rights Commission in future.

It noted that the suggestion had been made that a new Commission might be funded from non-Government sources and that it would not want to deter a move towards a non-statutory, private-financed body if its role was limited to functions such as public education and advice to individuals. A non-statutory body could not, however, absorb any of the functions of the existing statutory bodies concerned with human rights.[8]

Debates in Parliament

The Human Rights Bill was introduced first into the House of Lords and had its Second Reading on 3 November 1997. It completed its passage through that House in February 1998.

The case for a Human Rights Commissioner or Commission was made forcefully by Labour, Liberal Democrat, Cross-Bench and a

Conservative Peer. Some speeches (and proposed new clauses) focused on the potential role of the Commission in securing access to justice, others on its wider education role in promoting a culture of rights and responsibilities. Some, not least Baroness Amos and Baroness Lockwood, (former chief executive and former Chair of the EOC, respectively) argued for a broad Commission embracing the EOC and CRE; others focused on the essential functions of the body regardless of its structure.

Ministers reiterated the Government's view that more thought needed to be given to the form which the Commission might take and its hope that the new Parliamentary Human Rights Committee might consider this issue as the subject of its first inquiry. It was suggested that the Committee itself would perform an important role in educating the public about the implications of the Act by holding inquiries with hearings throughout the country. The Government wanted to see a change in culture, not least in public bodies.

The proposal that a decision should be deferred until after the Commission had been considered by a future Parliamentary Human Rights Committee was unattractive for three reasons. First, the plan to establish the Parliamentary Committee had not yet reached the drawing board. Delaying the establishment of a Commission until after the Committee had considered it would therefore inevitably mean a long delay.

Secondly, the greatest need for the Commission's work would be in the early stages of incorporation. This is when public bodies would be in most need of advice and guidance on good practice and when legal advisers would most need a source of expertise on Strasbourg jurisprudence, and on developing case law in the UK. Lord Holme:

> Surely the need for a Commission is at the beginning of this process, to take up cases to test the law, to encourage and assist individuals in a new area for the British courts and to promote good practice; in short to make the whole process work.[9]

Finally, while the Government was right to argue that a period of consultation was needed before a Commission could be established, it was argued that this could be organised by a Human Rights Commissioner appointed with that task as a primary responsibility within his or her first year of appointment.

This latter proposal was first suggested to IPPR by the Data Protection Registrar, Elizabeth France:

> nothing will evolve over time if the Human Rights Commissioner is not charged with achieving structural change. Perhaps a 'first term remit' for the Commissioner should be to review and recommend change to the current structure for protecting rights.[10]

Paul Stinchcombe MP, one of a number of Labour and Liberal Democrat MPs who raised the need for a Commission during the passage of the Human Rights Bill through the Commons, similarly argued:

> ...the best way for the Government to achieve progress would be by appointing a human rights commissioner soon, to push the agenda forward.[11]

Mr. Stinchcombe subsequently tabled an Early Day Motion which gained the support of 69 MPs:

> *That this House welcomes the priority which the Government has given to incorporation of the European Convention on Human Rights into domestic law and its willingness to discuss the establishment of a human rights commission or commissioner; expresses its firm belief that a statutory body will be needed from the beginning to promote awareness of the Act and to assist individuals who believe that their rights have been infringed; therefore urges the Government to consider the early appointment of a human rights commissioner with a specific remit to undertake those functions; and proposes that the commissioner should, after wide consultation, advise the Government and the proposed parliamentary human rights committee on the long-term options for a broader human rights commission and its potential relationship with existing statutory bodies.*

In the absence of a Human Rights Commissioner, the Government was urged to take the lead itself in consulting the existing bodies about the form which the Commission might take. Baroness Lockwood asked the Lord Chancellor to give his agreement in principle to having a

Commission and then to issue a consultative document on how best that might be achieved:

>...so as to maximise the full impact of the new Bill and at the same time to ensure that we do not lose out on any of the existing legislation and the work that the respective commissions are doing.[12]

and Baroness Amos asked the Government to:

>take the lead and consult on the options with respect to the creation of a human rights commission and build the consensus which they have rightly identified as being desirable.[13]

Northern Ireland

The debate on human rights protection in Northern Ireland is taking place within a very different context and historical background. Northern Ireland's small statutory advisory body, the Standing Advisory Commission on Human Rights, has long argued that its powers are inadequate to fulfil the functions which are needed and first raised the question whether a Commissioner for Human Rights should be appointed in its Discussion Paper *Bill of Rights* in 1976. Unlike in Britain, there has been cross party consensus that a Bill of Rights is needed in Northern Ireland for some time.

The need for a Human Rights Commission in Northern Ireland was on the agenda of the peace talks, resulting in a decision in the Agreement signed on 10 April 1998 that a Commission should be established 'with membership from Northern Ireland reflecting the community balance'. It will be independent of government and its principal functions were set out in the Agreement (see chapter 4). The Northern Ireland Bill, to implement the Agreement, began its passage through Parliament in July 1998. The Irish Government also undertook to establish a Commission with a similar mandate and it was agreed that there would be a committee of representatives from the two Commissions to consider issues relevant to the island of Ireland.

Northern Ireland has its own equality commissions, operating in parallel to their British counterparts - the Equal Opportunities

Commission (NI), the newly established Commission for Racial Equality (NI) and Disability Council (NI). In addition it has the Fair Employment Commission, enforcing the most robust piece of anti-discrimination legislation in the UK, covering religious and political discrimination in Northern Ireland only.

In March 1998, the Secretary of State for Northern Ireland published a White Paper, *Partnership for Equality*,[14] which announced that further legislation would be introduced to strengthen the role of the public sector in promoting equality of opportunity. A new public body would be needed to set standards for new statutory schemes, to monitor their implementation and investigate complaints that they had not been appropriately applied. The most rational organisational solution, it suggested, would be to bring the existing Northern Ireland equality commissions together into a single, unified, Equality Commission:

> to enable their work to be greatly extended into a new area, a positive engagement with the public sector to promote equality of opportunity in a broad sense.[15]

Provision for the Equality Commission was subsequently included in the Northern Ireland Bill.

Disability Rights Commission

A parallel debate has meanwhile been taking place in Britain and Northern Ireland: that on the structure and functions of the proposed Disability Rights Commission. In contrast to the Government's position on a UK Human Rights Commission, it has committed itself firmly to establishing a body to promote and enforce a strengthened Disability Discrimination Act. In November 1997 it established a taskforce of organisations and individuals to advise the responsible Minister in the Department for Education and Employment on the form which legislative proposals might take. At the taskforce's meeting in March 1998, it agreed the outline of that Commission's structure, powers and functions; a model similar to that of the CRE and EOC but with some modifications because of the particular nature of disability discrimination and in order to take account of criticisms made of the 1970s commission model. The speed with which the Minister wanted the taskforce to come to agreement reflected his wish, and theirs, that provision be made for the new Commission in the legislative programme to be announced in November 1998.

Information Commissioner

One final Government proposal completes the setting for this report: the intention to appoint an Information Commissioner to enforce the proposed Freedom of Information Act. A White Paper in November, *Your Right to Know*, proposed the creation of this new statutory authority with powers to enforce compliance with his or her rulings that information held by public authorities, or private bodies fulfilling public functions, should (or should not) be disclosed. This development indicates the Government's readiness to create new statutory bodies if convinced of the need to do so. It also raises the question what his or her relationship might be with a future Human Rights Commission which embraced certain existing statutory bodies in the human rights field. The Parliamentary Ombudsman has proposed that all of the individual complaints authorities should be brought within an overarching Information Commission to provide a one-stop-shop for complainants; a suggestion endorsed by the Select Committee on Public Administration in May 1998.

This report

In this report we address the questions which the Government has raised in relation to a Human Rights Commission in Britain and in Northern Ireland and put the issues within their international context. In the chapters which follow we make the case for the establishment of a UK Human Rights Commission, set out the responsibilities which it and the Northern Ireland Human Rights Commission should have, consider the options for their structure and suggest mechanisms for their accountability to Parliament and to the public. We consider whether there should be separate arrangements for Scotland, England and Wales, and suggest what the UK body would cost.

Chapter 2 describes the existing mechanisms for protecting human rights within Whitehall, Parliament, the courts and some key public bodies. In the context of the rights which will be enforceable when the European Convention has been incorporated, it identifies the limitations of the existing arrangements, demonstrating why a new body is needed in the UK to fulfil certain clearly identified roles. Chapter 3 looks abroad to the guidelines on national human rights institutions set down by the UN and then to the varied experience of these bodies in countries throughout the world. Chapter 4 reviews the possible functions of the new UK body and the Northern Ireland Commission, concluding with a clear recommendation on the functions which should be considered essential.

Chapter 5 considers the options for the Commission's structure - whether there should be separate bodies in Scotland, England and Wales; and whether the Human Rights Commission should be separate from the existing discrimination Commissions or should bring them within its umbrella. It explains the relationship which the Commission could have with the Government and with Parliament; and advocates statutory Advisory Councils as a mechanism for ensuring that the Commission remains in touch with the opinion of outside bodies with an interest in its work. Finally it considers the internal structure of the UK Commission, the means of appointment and dismissal of its members and a possible departmental structure. It concludes by setting out the potential cost of the UK Commission in its first year, giving the details of that costing in Appendix 3. The Conclusion summarises our arguments and recommendations.

It is our hope that the report will help to clarify the issues which the Government has said require further consideration and foster the debate which is needed in order to build a consensus on the way forward.

Endnotes

1. Second Reading of the Human Rights Bill, HL, 3 November 1997, Hansard col 1256.

2. Vienna Declaration and Programme of Action, Part 1, para 36.

3. Recommendations No.R (97) 14 of the Committee of Ministers to Member States on the Establishment of Independent National Human Rights Institutions, adopted on 30 September 1967 at the 602nd meeting of the Minister's Deputies. The full text of The Recommendation is given in Appendix 2.

4. Foreign Office Minister Tony Lloyd MP addressing the CHRI/IPPR Conference on Commonwealth Human Rights Institutions in London on 16 October 1997. Details of funding confirmed in letter from the Minister to IPPR dated 5 January 1998.

5. *Bringing Rights Home, Labour's plans to incorporate the European Convention on Human Rights into UK law. A Consultation Paper.* Jack Straw MP, Shadow Home Secretary and Paul Boateng MP, Shadow Minister for the Lord Chancellor's Department. December 1996.

6. Report of the Joint Consultative Committee on Constitutional Reform, para 22. 1997.

7. The Constitution Unit (1996) *Human Rights Legislation,* The Constitution Unit pages 78-86.

8. Chapter 3, 'Improving Compliance with the Convention Rights', *Right Brought Home: The Human Rights Bill,* Home Office CM 3782, October 1997.

9. Second Reading of the Human Rights Bill, HL, 3 November 1997, Hansard col 1258.

10. Letter to the authors, 19 December 1997.

11. Second Reading of the Human Rights Bill, HC, 16 February 1998, col. 818.

12. Committee Stage of the Human Rights Bill, HL, 24 November 1997, Hansard col 847-8.

13. Second Reading, HL, *ibid,* col 1249

14. Northern Ireland Office *Partnership for Equality,* March 1998. Cm 3890.

15. White Paper, *ibid,* para 4.12.

2. Human Rights Protection in the UK

The UK has ratified, and is thus bound by, a wide range of international human rights standards, only some of which are enforceable in the UK's own courts.

Incorporation of the European Convention (ECHR) will bring within UK law the rights contained in one important, if limited, human rights instrument. That Convention is part of an international system established after the Second World War to protect individuals from the abuse of power, a system which sets minimum standards for civil, political, social and economic rights but usually has only weak mechanisms at the international level to enforce them. The UK's decision to incorporate the ECHR will make the civil and political rights it contains enforceable in courts and tribunals throughout the UK, not only at the more distant European Court of Human Rights in Strasbourg.

Providing legally enforceable rights, however, is insufficient. Governments also need to provide:

● *Access to justice:* to have access to the courts, individuals may need specialist advice and financial assistance.

● *Prevention:* procedures are needed within Whitehall, Parliament and public bodies to avoid measures being introduced which infringe rights.

● *Awareness:* steps need to be taken to promote awareness of human rights principles so that people adopt those standards in their daily lives - at school, at work, within the family and in public life.

These mechanisms of prevention and promotion need to reflect the UK's wide range of obligations under international human rights law - like the UN Convention on the Rights of the Child and the Geneva Refugee Convention - all of which are legally binding on the UK. They should not be limited to those rights contained in the ECHR.

This chapter assesses the extent to which the systems in the UK fulfil these requirements. It concludes that there are gaps in the system which need to be rectified by establishing a new statutory body, a Human Rights Commission.

The importance of human rights

Only during the last fifty years have nations sought to co-operate effectively to protect human rights. The concept of natural or fundamental rights was first developed in the 18th Century but it was not until the world had witnessed the horrors of Nazism that nations were motivated to agree a set of binding principles of human liberty and freedom. At the same time they began to establish international mechanisms to monitor and enforce compliance with those standards in the belief that the combined effect of these efforts would help to prevent the return of tyranny and inhumanity.

Much of the impetus for this movement came from those who had fought against Hitler and his allies. Their ideas about human rights reflected a social and political philosophy built around representative democracy, the rule of law, respect for human dignity and the importance of political and religious pluralism. The right to life and freedom from torture, inhuman treatment or slavery, for example, had vivid relevance to those times. Freedom to express political beliefs or to practice personal religion without state interference assumed similar significance.

Post-War developments in the field of human rights have not, however, sprung from a narrow libertarian philosophy. Proponents have also acknowledged the need for competing rights to be balanced with each other and for social or collective interests to be respected. The ECHR thus allows some of the rights it contains to be curtailed where this can be shown to be necessary 'in a democratic society' in the interests of national security, public health or for the protection of the rights and freedoms of others. States are not just expected to refrain from acting in ways which violate these obligations but to take positive steps to ensure that the rights and freedoms are given effect.

More than fifty years after the Second World War it remains as important to protect human rights. In a multi-cultural society which values diversity, the need for a common set of fundamental standards is essential, while the enhanced ability of the state to exercise control over the individual requires safeguards to ensure that liberty and democracy are protected.

At one extreme, we have seen in former Yugoslavia and in Northern Ireland how death and destruction can result from communal hatred, suspicion and strife. In Britain, racist assaults afflict whole communities while domestic violence blights the lives of many women. Malpractice by public officials, combined with deep-seated unfairness in the criminal justice system, have caused a series of miscarriages of justice and the wrongful imprisonment of those convicted in error.

The physical and mental abuse of vulnerable citizens living in institutions - children in care, the elderly or people with a mental illness or learning disability - continue to be exposed. Technological developments have given those in Government and commerce - and an ever more intrusive media - the opportunity to trespass into areas of life formerly regarded as private and confidential. Unfair discrimination persists in the workplace and elsewhere for those apparently protected by the law[1] and for those who still have no rights under it.[2]

It was to avoid such treatment that the international system of human rights protection was developed, bolstered by specific rights codified in domestic law.

International and domestic law

The term human rights covers not only civil and political rights but also social, economic and cultural rights. For the UK, there are three potential sources for such standards:

- International law (including the ECHR)

- European Community law

- UK domestic law

International law

Human rights have been defined in a number of binding international treaties which now constitute an extensive body of standards and procedures. The key instruments ratified by, and hence binding on, the UK are those of the United Nations (UN), the Council of Europe and the International Labour Organisation (ILO).[3]

Only in relation to the Council of Europe's Convention on Human Rights (ECHR) is there a court to enforce the rights in the treaty. The ECHR was drafted with the assistance of British lawyers and entered into force in 1953. It contains a wide range of civil and political rights and, in most cases, the grounds on which they may be restricted.

The key provisions of the ECHR

- the obligation for all parties to secure for everyone within their jurisdiction the rights and freedoms provided for in the Convention (Article 1)

- the right to life (Article 2)

- freedom from torture or inhuman and degrading treatment and punishment (Article 3)

- freedom from slavery, servitude or forced or compulsory labour (Article 4)

- the right to liberty and security of the person (Article 5)

- the right to a fair trial (Article 6)

- freedom from retrospective criminal offences and punishment (Article 7)

- the right to respect for private and family life, for home and for correspondence (Article 8)

- freedom of religion (Article 9)

- freedom of expression (Article 10)

- freedom of assembly and association (Article 11)

- the right to marry and to found a family (Article 12)

- the right to an effective remedy (Article 13)

- freedom from discrimination in respect of these rights (Article 14)

If an individual believes that his or her rights under the Convention have been infringed, they have, since 1966, been able to take their case to the Commission and the Court of Human Rights in Strasbourg. Legal aid is available for such proceedings and numerous complaints have been lodged, heard and decided, many from this country.[4]

In a significant proportion of cases the Court has decided that the UK breached the terms of the Convention, requiring changes to law or policy concerning the rights of prisoners,[5] detained psychiatric patients,[6] homosexuals,[7] children in care,[8] newspaper publishers and journalists,[9] and applicants for legal aid.[10] These cases have demonstrated the importance of an international system for calling governments to account and that breaches of human rights in the UK are to be found across a wide range of policy areas.

The ICCPR

The principal UN Convention protecting civil and political rights is the International Covenant on Civil and Political Rights which was ratified by the UK in 1976. It covers a wider range of rights than the ECHR including a free-standing non-discrimination provision which, unlike the ECHR, covers the key area of employment. Compliance with the Covenant is supervised at the international level by the United Nations Human Rights Committee, a body of independent experts elected by member states.

The Committee studies reports submitted by each government every five years. The government is then questioned by the Committee in public hearings. In a recent report on the UK, the Human Rights Committee expressed its concern about such matters as prison conditions, the exercise of police powers in relation to ethnic minorities and the treatment of illegal immigrants, asylum seekers and potential deportees.

In addition to this limited form of supervision, some governments permit their citizens to approach the Committee direct with a complaint of a breach of the Covenant. The decisions of the Committee have no legal force but carry moral and political authority. Since the United Kingdom, almost alone among its European partners, does not allow individuals to make such complaints, its accountability under this Convention is limited to scrutiny of its periodic reports. The Government is currently considering whether to give individuals the right to lodge complaints.

Conventions on discrimination: CERD and CEDAW

The International Convention on the Elimination of All Forms of Racial Discrimination (CERD) was ratified by the UK in 1969. Under this

Convention, racial discrimination and segregation are prohibited together with racist propaganda. Governments agree to promote equal rights and effective remedies against racism and to take action to combat prejudice and to promote 'understanding, tolerance and friendship' between races and ethnic groups.

The commitments in CERD are more extensive and more detailed than the limited anti-discrimination provisions of the ECHR and ICCPR. An expert Committee considers reports from each country every two years. Where a State permits it — again the UK has not done so — individual complaints can also be made to the Committee.

A similar system operates in relation to the Convention on the Elimination of All Forms of Discrimination against Women (CEDAW) which was ratified by the UK in 1986. Four yearly periodic reports on each country are considered. There is at present no procedure for the consideration of individual complaints. Under CEDAW, States undertake to 'pursue by all appropriate means and without delay a policy of eliminating discrimination against women' and commit themselves to a series of detailed measures to achieve that objective.

In practice, reporting on UK practice to these committees has been undertaken by the Foreign Office with little involvement or awareness by outside bodies. The detailed requirements of the Conventions are probably unfamiliar even to many of those working in the equality field. They are rarely used as a yardstick by which to judge government policies on race or gender equality. Neither employers nor public bodies use the standards in these Conventions to guide their equal opportunities policies. Their impact on the UK must therefore be deemed to be marginal.

The UN Convention on the Rights of the Child (CRC)

The UN Convention on the Rights of the Child was ratified by the UK in 1991. It differs from earlier Conventions in the prominence which it gives to rights within the private sphere of family life. The Convention requires that primacy should be given to the best interests of the child and contains a range of civil and social rights including the child's right to have his or her views taken into account and respected, a right to protection from abuse, to social security and to freedom from economic exploitation. Periodic reports on each of the countries which have ratified the Convention are considered by an expert Committee every five years.

The Committee on the Rights of the Child encourages alternative reports to be submitted by non-governmental organisations and a comprehensive report on the situation in the UK was submitted by the Children's Rights Development Unit to the first review in 1994. That report detailed the many areas of UK law, policy and practice which do not conform to the Convention and was instrumental in the UK receiving a critical report from the Committee.[11] Its findings were never discussed in Parliament, however, and the Government of the day showed little inclination to address the problems which the Committee identified. In these circumstances, the international enforcement machinery for such Conventions cannot be said to be an effective mechanism.

Social and economic rights

The Conventions which focus entirely on social, economic or cultural rights, such as the International Covenant on Economic, Social and Cultural Rights (ICESCR) and the Council of Europe's Social Charter, are often framed differently - as aspirations for policy rather than as enforceable rights. The latter requires governments to pursue 'by all appropriate means' the policy aims in the Convention, such as that appropriate facilities shall be provide for vocational training and that social and medical assistance shall be available for those without adequate resources.

The Charter's impact is monitored by a Committee of Independent Experts which considers reports every two years from each government and publishes its own report on each country's compliance with its Charter obligations. Reports are then passed to the Council of Ministers which has the power to issue recommendations to each government.

Limitations of the international system

It is clear from this summary that all of the human rights treaties except the ECHR are unenforceable by UK citizens because, under UK law, treaties do not automatically become part of domestic law. Methods for international review and monitoring are limited in what they can achieve and operate at a political and diplomatic level not judicially. Such systems can appear remote and inaccessible to all but experienced international lobbyists, NGOs, lawyers or tenacious citizens.

The system of monitoring by expert committees on the basis of

periodic reports weads an insufficient sanction to persuade the
government and public authorities to scrutinise their policies, practices
and proposals in order to ensure that these comply with the
Conventions, even though they have the status of binding international
law. Consequently, the requirements of these Conventions, and many
others which are not mentioned here, are not generally known or widely
acknowledged either in Government or wider society.

European Community law

Unlike international treaties, EC law does become part of UK domestic
law so that the courts can enforce it in cases coming before them. EC
law is found in the treaties establishing the Community, in its legislation
(Regulations and Directives) and in decisions of the European Court of
Justice (ECtJ).

A distinct catalogue of defined human rights has not been included
in any of the EC treaties. Article F of the Maastricht Treaty (TEU) does
provide that:

> The Union shall respect fundamental rights, as guaranteed by
> the European Convention for the Protection of Human Rights
> and Fundamental Freedoms...

but it is not justiciable. The Treaty of Amsterdam has gone further and
expanded the jurisdiction of the Court of Justice so as to deal with some
claims that a member state has breached the ECHR and a new
committee of the European Parliament is to be established to scrutinise
EC laws for compliance with that Convention.

Despite the absence of specific Treaty provisions on human rights,
EC legislation has in practice provided some protection for individual
rights. These differ, however, from traditional human rights in two
ways. First, these entitlements are acquired only by those possessing
citizenship of a member country. Secondly, the EC has been and
remains predominantly concerned with creating and maintaining an
economic and commercial market. Rights which have been provided at
Community level are therefore linked to the workplace or to achieving
full participation in the EC's labour market. When considered by the
ECtJ they must be balanced with the economic and commercial
imperatives of the Single European Market.

This is not to say that such rights have never corresponded with accepted civil or social rights. The EC Directives on Equal Pay and Equal Treatment, for example, have fundamentally affected the development of sex discrimination and equal pay law throughout the Union in ways which British governments might never have contemplated.

The Amsterdam Treaty has further extended the law making powers of the European Community to measures designed to combat discrimination on grounds of race or ethnic origin, sexual orientation, age, disability and religion or belief although it may be some time before the European Commission drafts legislation on these matters which is acceptable to every member state.

Domestic law

In some countries, treaty obligations binding in international law also form part of that nation's domestic law. If that were the case in the UK then provisions in Conventions such as the ICCPR and the ECHR would already be directly enforceable in our domestic courts. In the UK, specific legislation must be enacted if treaties are to have effect in domestic law, as indeed the Government is doing with the ECHR.

The UK has, on occasion, adapted its laws to include, in effect, some of the human rights standards by which it is bound at an international level. A number of statutory provisions can be said to reflect those standards - some more effectively than others.[12] The most notable are the laws against discrimination on grounds of sex, race and disability, and on grounds of political opinion and religion in Northern Ireland.[13]

Prior to incorporation of the European Convention, English law has not however been 'rights based', unlike other legal systems which have written constitutions and Bills of Rights or where treaties form part of domestic law. Changes in our system of legislation and common law have been piecemeal. As a result there are significant gaps in the human rights protection available to people in the UK[14] (only some of which will be remedied by the Human Rights Act).

Anti-discrimination legislation, for instance, is full of gaps and anomalies. In Great Britain religious discrimination is not prohibited; nor is racial discrimination by officials (such as police or prison officers) generally unlawful. Throughout the UK discrimination on grounds of age remains lawful.

The common law fails to provide effective protection for the public from unwarranted intrusions into their private lives from the press, public officials or commercial interests. It similarly fails to protect prisoners, detained psychiatric patients and children detained in secure accommodation from inhuman and degrading treatment or punishment resulting, for example, from improper methods of restraint, solitary confinement or the giving of treatment for non-therapeutic reasons.

Scrutiny in Whitehall and Parliament [15]

One key criterion for an effective domestic system of human rights protection is procedure within government and Parliament which will scrutinise draft legislation and existing provisions to ensure that they conform to international human rights standards. In the UK there is evidence that these procedures are inadequate: of the 29 ECHR judgements up to November 1991 finding the UK in breach of the Convention, 22 involved breaches within primary or secondary legislation itself.[16]

Whitehall

The scrutiny of policy proposals within Whitehall is governed by *Questions of Procedure for Ministers* and by the *Civil Service Code,* the administrative guidance given, respectively, to Ministers and to civil servants as to the proper conduct of Government business. The provisions of the Civil Service Code which came into force on 1 January 1996 summarise the Minister's duty to '..comply with the law, including international law and treaty obligations...' and state that civil servants are under a parallel duty, framed in precisely the same terms.

Rejecting the need for new scrutiny procedures, the previous government stated:

> Ministers putting proposals to Cabinet or a Ministerial Committee are already required by Questions of Procedure for Ministers to cover, where appropriate, the impact of the European Convention on Human Rights. In addition, where a department is considering legislation, it is required to ensure that its plans are compatible with the international human rights obligations of the United Kingdom, including the European Convention on Human Rights in particular.[17]

Civil service lawyers are thus required to scrutinise legislative proposals to ensure that they comply with such obligations. In practice, their primary concern is obligations under the ECHR, being the only Convention with an effective enforcement machinery. 'Strasbourg proofing', as it is known, has operated on the basis of risk avoidance rather than as a pro-active approach towards implementing human rights standards. No priority has been given in the past to integrating those standards into mainstream departmental policy-making.

Nor do the present arrangements alert Parliament to any potential breaches of the UK's international legal obligations. Legal opinions offered to Ministers on the compliance of their proposals with international law remain confidential, as do the reasons which the Government may have for accepting or rejecting the advice given.

Scrutiny in Northern Ireland

In one respect, matters are handled differently in Northern Ireland. Since 1993, *Guidelines on Policy Appraisal and Fair Treatment* (PAFT) have been issued within the Northern Ireland Office and all Northern Ireland departments. The effect has been to create a more systematic and open process of 'equality proofing' for government policies and legislative proposals, as well as for service delivery. Each department must publish an annual report detailing any new policies or proposals introduced during the previous twelve months and the impact upon them of the fair treatment principles defined in the guidance.

As far as *international* human rights standards are concerned, the impact of the PAFT process may be more apparent than real. Although the primary guidance refers explicitly to the need to have regard to human rights guarantees at an international level, the 1995 Annual Report for PAFT made no mention of the requirements of the Convention on the Elimination of Racial Discrimination, to give one example, despite frequent references to new proposals for race equality legislation in Northern Ireland.

A White Paper *Partnership for Equality*,[18] published in March 1998, effectively proposes to put the PAFT process on a statutory footing and apply it to all public bodies, not only central government departments. A single Equality Commission is being established to monitor and enforce the process. The relationship of the process of equality proofing to that of 'Strasbourg proofing' is not clear.

Parliamentary scrutiny

Within Parliament, there is currently no discrete procedure which ensures that the human rights implications of draft legislation are scrutinised. There is no Select Committee with specific responsibility in this area and the committees which scrutinise delegated legislation are apparently prevented from carrying out any scrutiny for conformity with ratified international treaties.[19] This situation is compounded by the fact that most Parliamentarians are inexpert in human rights law and do not have access to expert legal opinion, unlike those representing the government.

The Government has suggested that Parliament might establish a Committee on Human Rights; either a Joint Committee of both Houses of Parliament or two separate committees. Whereas Labour's consultation paper on incorporation, prior to the election, foresaw a role for that committee in scrutinising draft legislation which 'was identified as having an impact on human rights issues', the White Paper makes no reference to this role. It suggests that the committee might conduct inquiries on a range of human rights issues relating to the European Convention and produce reports so as to assist the Government in deciding what action to take. It might also range more widely, examining issues relating to the other international obligations of the UK such as proposals to accept new rights under other human rights treaties.[20]

The impact of incorporation on scrutiny

When the Human Rights Act comes into force, the compatibility of the government's decisions and policies, and legislation itself will, from time to time, be challenged in court. The importance to government of obtaining sound opinion as to the meaning and application of the Convention will thus increase significantly. Ministers contemplating new measures will not be able to count on a delay of many years before these measures are considered in the light of the ECHR. They will need to be sure from the outset that they are acting within the law.

The Human Rights Act will require the Minister in charge of a Bill in either House of Parliament to publish a written statement to the effect either that the provisions of the Bill are compatible with the Convention rights or that, although the Minister is unable to make such a statement, the Government nevertheless wishes the House to proceed with the Bill.

This new procedure will enhance the priority given to 'Strasbourg proofing' within government and draw to the attention of Parliament the human rights implications of each Bill. A statement of compatibility without any supporting analysis explaining how that conclusion was reached, however, will not alter the disadvantage at which Parliamentarians currently find themselves when seeking to challenge such Ministerial assurances. This is because, in many cases, a provision is neither clearly in breach, nor in conformity, to the Convention. It is often a question of judgement and Parliamentarians need to know how that judgement was arrived at. Parliamentarians will need an independent source of expert advice on the international human rights standards if they are to question Ministers effectively.

Public bodies with human rights responsibilities

There are a number of public bodies which have responsibility for promoting and enforcing certain human rights standards. The best known of these are the Commissions associated with the anti-discrimination laws but there are also bodies concerned with the conditions under which people are detained as well as one statutory body concerned with privacy standards. There is only one small organisation which considers itself to have a general responsibility in relation to human rights standards and its remit is restricted to Northern Ireland: the Standing Advisory Commission on Human Rights (SACHR). SACHR is to be replaced by Northern Ireland's Human Rights Commission but its experience is instructive.

Standing Advisory Commission on Human Rights

SACHR was established by the Northern Ireland Constitution Act 1973. Its statutory role is narrowly defined - to advise the Secretary of State on the adequacy and effectiveness of laws against discrimination on grounds of religion or politics - a definition which does not even include the term 'human rights'.[21] Members of the Commission are appointed by the Secretary of State for Northern Ireland.

SACHR has a part-time Chairman and its members include the Northern Ireland Ombudsman and the Chairpersons of the Fair Employment Commission and of the Equal Opportunities Commission (NI). It is a small body [22] with five full time staff, only one of whom is expected to have any specialist knowledge of human rights law.

The Commission has regularly recommended to the Secretary of State that its limited statutory remit be extended in scope. In the absence of such reform, it has in practice been permitted to undertake work beyond its remit across a range of human rights concerns including the non-jury Diplock courts, a Bill of Rights for Northern Ireland, divorce law, homosexual law reform, disability and education. One long-standing member of SACHR estimated that 90 per cent of its work has been undertaken outside of its statutory remit. Its research and recommendations in the sphere of discrimination and inequality have often been highly regarded: its 1987 Report on Fair Employment was instrumental in the subsequent legislation which strengthened existing measures to tackle religious and political discrimination in the workplace,[23] and its 1997 report *Employment Equality: Building for the Future* [24] equally had a significant influence on the recent White Paper, *Partnership for Equality.*

SACHR's role, nevertheless, remains an advisory one. Ministers of successive governments have regularly ignored its advice and on occasions have not even consulted the body before introducing controversial measures with significant implications for human rights, for example the Sinn Fein broadcasting ban or restrictions on the right of silence for suspects.

SACHR has no executive powers and is unable to provide advice or assistance to members of the public; nor does it have the powers necessary to conduct an inquiry into matters causing public concern.[25] It cannot initiate legal proceedings on its own behalf nor intervene in another party's action to provide expert opinion, although it has in practice provided a written opinion to the European Court of Human Rights. SACHR does not have any independent corporate legal status and regards itself 'in formal governmental terms' to be 'within the Northern Ireland Office, which is responsible for organising and financing its work'.[26] An independent report commissioned by SACHR and published in 1990 found that the Commission had:

> ...arguably reached the limits of its collective achievement; ...was not a strong force to be reckoned with in the political arena of Northern Ireland; ..... had not adopted a strong campaigning role; [and] that its exclusion from consideration of individual complaints had militated against wider direct involvement in the community.[27]

The report recommended that the statutory remit of the Commission needed to be broadened substantially to permit a real measure of co-ordination of the activities of other human rights agencies in Northern Ireland. It further proposed that the Chairperson should always be legally qualified; that the members of the Commission should have the knowledge and experience to enable them to make a substantial contribution to its work and that it should have a larger staff.

SACHR accepted this assessment:

> ...as a purely advisory body the Commission is unable to take any decisive action on matters of major concern to it. Related to this is the Commission's uncertain status as a non-corporate body attached to and in practice dependent upon the Northern Ireland Office for all its staffing and administrative requirements. This advisory and dependent status does not prevent the Commission from expressing its own independent views with whatever force it can muster and the Commission wishes to place on record that it has never been prevented by the Northern Ireland Office from publicising its views on any matter. But it does prevent the Commission from initiating or even assisting in the initiation of formal proceedings in respect of matters of concern to it.

> ...Since the Commission lacks any separate legal personality and has no independent budget, research contracts sponsored by it must be entered into formally by the Northern Ireland Office which exercises ultimate control over their financing, as with all other aspects of the Commission's operations.

Noting that the international practice of human rights agencies lent further support to the view that a body without independent status or power of independent initiative is unlikely to be able to play a major role in the protection and promotion of human rights, it concluded that SACHR:

> must have greater independence and freedom of action if it is to carry out effectively its role in protecting human rights in Northern Ireland.[28]

SACHR argued that it would need substantial changes to its constitution, its statutory role and its level of resources if it were to be expected to have a significant influence. It did not seek to provide advice and assistance to individuals nor to enforce human rights standards.

Despite SACHR's recognition of the limitations of its dependent status, its submissions to international supervisory bodies such as the UN Human Rights Committee and to the Committee on Torture begin with the words: 'The Standing Advisory Commission on Human Rights is an independent statutory body..'[29]

Equal treatment Commissions

There are five Commissions in the UK responsible for the promotion and enforcement of equality legislation: two separate Commissions for Racial Equality (CRE) tackle race discrimination in Britain and in Northern Ireland respectively; two Equal Opportunity Commissions (EOC) respectively for Britain and for Northern Ireland enforce sex equality laws on pay and discrimination; while the Fair Employment Commission (FEC) is responsible for combating discrimination on grounds of religious or political belief in employment in Northern Ireland. Laws prohibiting discrimination on grounds of disability were introduced in 1995 throughout the UK and the Government has announced its intention to establish a Disability Rights Commission. The existing National Disability Council, and its equivalent in Northern Ireland, have an advisory role only and would be replaced by the new Commission.

Commissioners of the existing multi-member Commissions are appointed by Ministers and take decisions on a collegiate basis. Because of the Commissions' responsibilities in the field of employment, employers' and employees' interests are reflected in the choice of Commissioners, with the CBI and the TUC each entitled to offer a nominee for appointment. The organisations rely almost entirely on Government funding although there is some private sponsorship of promotional activities and some European Union funding for research.

The equality Commissions attract many inquiries from individuals seeking their assistance to investigate and pursue complaints of discrimination. The absence of legal aid in Industrial Tribunals (where most discrimination cases are heard) and the improved chances of success which accompany the expert assistance given by the

Commissions, combine to maintain high levels of demand for assistance.

Each of the bodies also has specific powers to investigate alleged discrimination and to take enforcement measures against it. These powers are designed to be used to tackle systemic discrimination rather than isolated breaches of the law. The Commissions can investigate named persons or organisations, can issue reports of such investigations and serve mandatory notices requiring action if they conclude that the law has been broken. Ancillary powers are available to the Commissions to secure co-operation with their investigation such as the power to call for documents or for the attendance of witnesses.[30] A person or body served with a non-discrimination notice and wishing to object has a right of appeal to the appropriate court or tribunal.

In addition to providing assistance to individuals, conducting investigations, undertaking research and public promotion, the bodies may monitor new policy and proposals for legislation and put a case to Ministers and to Parliament for changes to the law.

The CRE was formed in 1976 by merging the Race Relations Board and the Community Relations Commission. This historical link with community relations is retained in the CRE's responsibility for the funding and co-ordination of race equality officers throughout Britain. Based in London, the Commission has established regional offices. Its published accounts (1997-98) show expenditure of £15m and a total staff complement of 214. Its counterpart in Northern Ireland was established in 1997. It had a budgeted income for 1997 of £0.45m and a total staff of 5.

The EOC (GB) is based in Manchester, with regional offices in Scotland and Wales. Its annual expenditure in 1997/8 was £6m and the number of staff in that year totalled 160. The equivalent figures for the EOC (NI) were £1.5m and 36. Both EOCs have exploited the opportunities for the strategic enforcement of sex equality laws.[31] They have also employed remedies provided by EU law, in part overcoming some of the weaknesses inherent in the UK statutes and their judicial interpretation.

The Fair Employment Commission took over and extended the responsibilities of the Fair Employment Agency, a Northern Ireland body which had been established in 1976 to combat employment discrimination on religious or political grounds. The FEC has a distinct profile and significantly greater powers than the other equality Commissions. Employers must register with the Commission and must monitor the make-up of their workforce on grounds covered by the Act. The Commission can require measures to encourage recruitment from under represented religious groups. This has led to calls for all of the equality Commissions to be equipped with similar powers and responsibilities if they are to be fully effective.[32] Because of its more extensive responsibilities - and the political prominence given to inequality in Northern Ireland - the FEC is better resourced than the other bodies in Northern Ireland. Its expenditure in 1995/6 was £2.95m and its staff during that year totalled 89.

The Fair Employment Act 1989 was recently the subject of a wide-ranging review by SACHR examining both the impact of the legislation and the FEC's effectiveness. That review was followed by the Government's White Paper *Partnership for Equality*, in March 1998. The Northern Ireland Bill replaces the separate Northern Ireland equality bodies with the Equality Commission proposed in that document.

Limits and opportunities

Much has been written about the weaknesses in the present system for combating discrimination, a situation arising in part from the piece-meal development of discrimination policy and law within the UK over a thirty-year period.

The mandate and powers of each Commission derive from their founding statutes which, in the main, focus on a fairly narrow concept of discrimination, both as to the grounds of discrimination and to the scope of protection given. Thus, discrimination in employment or in the provision of goods and services due to religion, age, sexual orientation or political opinion are not yet prohibited throughout the UK. Consequently, the CRE can investigate race discrimination but not discrimination on grounds of religion, despite the close links often found in practice between them.

Discrimination on grounds of disability is illegal in defined situations but no public body yet exists to enforce the law. The Government is committed to establishing a Commission but the extent to which it will also strengthen the Act is not yet clear.

The equality Commissions are also precluded from taking up non-discrimination human rights issues, even where closely related to the issues within their mandate. The Equal Opportunities Commissions, for instance, are unable to take up the issue of domestic violence towards women nor practices which amount to 'degrading treatment' which will become unlawful when the Human Rights Act comes into force.

All of the Commissions (except the FEC) have found their jurisdiction and powers restricted in a series of judgements in the higher court.[33] The CRE, for example, has been prevented from investigating racial discrimination by public officials such as immigration officers and prison staff.[34] 'Indirect' discrimination under both sex and race legislation is restrictively interpreted.[35] The ability of the Commissions to investigate and to deal with systemic discrimination is greatly hampered by their lack of proper powers of enforcement and by their restricted power to take representative actions. There is also no requirement on employers to monitor their work force on grounds of race or gender.

In its reviews of the Act, the CRE has repeatedly drawn these and other weaknesses to the attention of the government of the day. It has called for wide-ranging reform of the legislation under which it operates to extend its powers to monitor and enforce equality of opportunity.[36] The EOCs have both made submissions to government, detailing similar weaknesses in their legislation.

Without amendment to their legislation when the ECHR is incorporated into domestic law, the Commissions will not have standing to pursue cases under the Convention, despite the fact that it contains a non-discrimination Article and will provide new prohibitions against discrimination on grounds of race or gender in important fields of government activity for the first time. If this difficulty were remedied by changes to the legal framework within which each Commission operates they would still be precluded by the terms of the Human Rights Act from initiating cases under that Act, but could provide legal assistance to a victim.

Some of the limitations on the Commissions arise, however, from their isolation as separate organisations. This has encouraged the impression that rights to equal treatment are minority concerns; that these bodies exist to protect the interests of particular social groups rather than promoting and enforcing human rights of concern to society as a whole.

The separation of the organisations also limits opportunities for combined action and the pooling of resources. Although Commissioners from each of the separate bodies have met twice a year to discuss matters of mutual concern (and have begun to do so more often recently), no formal framework exists to ensure that the Commissions work effectively together, pooling their resources and experience where appropriate.

The promotion of equality standards relating to race and sex, for example, cover similar issues, employ similar methods and are directed to the same audience. Yet the Commissions rarely join forces to provide single publications such as codes of practice covering all forms of discrimination. There are also limits to the extent to which they are allowed to share information relating to particular companies or cases. No database is produced concerning all of the discrimination cases, despite the relevance of cases on gender, say, to those on race.

These limitations may, according to a Consultative Paper circulated some years ago by the CRE, dissipate effort and reduce the effectiveness of the Commissions.[37] Research exercises covering all forms of discrimination are not commissioned and the existence of separate bodies reduces the effectiveness of strategic law enforcement by restricting the range of material from which to select and test legal issues arising in more than one area of discrimination law.

The present system also leads to problems of access for the public. There are many situations where a person has experienced discrimination on more than one ground or is unsure of the reason they have been discriminated against. Cases of multiple discrimination, for example where an individual has been the victim of sex and race discrimination, cannot be pursued by any single body able to deal with every legal aspect of the matter.[38] Instead of a 'one-stop-shop' the person has to approach separate Commissions, based in different cities, for advice and for support; Commissions which in practice may adopt different criteria for giving that assistance. The same difficulty affects employers. These concerns are addressed more fully in Chapter 5.

There has been much discussion about reform. A paper published by Justice and the Runnymede Trust canvassed options, including the establishment of an Equality Commissioner and a single Equality Act.[39]

Detention supervision bodies

There are four groups of people which can have their right to liberty curtailed by being detained in some form of custody or custodial care: migrants, prisoners, children and psychiatric patients.

The European Convention for the Prevention of Torture and Inhuman and Degrading Treatment or Punishment (1987) is one of the international instruments which sets standards for such detention in the UK and the Committee established under that treaty visits UK institutions in which people are detained in order to monitor the conditions in which they are held. Such visits are infrequent and cover only a fraction of the total number of facilities.

The Committee has no capacity for dealing with individual complaints which are expected to be the responsibility of domestic bodies. Only limited protection has yet been established at a domestic level and the procedures which exist are mainly designed to protect the interests and welfare of detained psychiatric patients. There are numerous weaknesses in the present system with bodies lacking essential powers or independence and protection being far from comprehensive.

Statutory bodies set up to regulate the detention of patients lack a human rights perspective. They owe their existence to a long tradition of paternalistic concerns for the welfare of patients unable to look after their own interests, rather than to a clear commitment to, and procedures for, defining and respecting individual rights.

The Mental Health Act Commission for England and Wales has, since 1983, been responsible for monitoring the conditions under which patients are detained for treatment under the Mental Health Act 1983 and for investigating complaints received from patients about how the Act was used or how they were treated. Being constituted as a special health authority, this Commission has limited independence and has no power to end the detention of a patient, even if it believes it to be unlawful.

The equivalent bodies in Northern Ireland and in Scotland have greater powers and independence. The Mental Welfare Commission in Scotland has a duty to investigate unlawful detention reported to it and has the power to discharge a patient where it decides that there are no longer grounds for detention.

For prisoners and those detained in police custody, arrangements are far less developed. A non-statutory Prisons Ombudsman has recently been established to receive and investigate complaints from prisoners arising from their detention. The Ombudsman's terms of reference and powers are defined by the Home Secretary who, under the previous administration, amended them to restrict the scope of investigations, without reference to Parliament. The Ombudsman is only able to recommend action to Ministers or to the officials responsible for the Prison Service.

The Police Complaints Authority in England and Wales supervises complaints of serious misconduct by police officers and decides if any disciplinary action should be taken. It has no powers of investigation itself; nor does it adjudicate discipline 'charges' – these remain the responsibility of the police themselves. For these reasons, the Authority is often seen as ineffectual when dealing with complaints of human rights abuses by the police. Similar arrangements apply in Northern Ireland, but in Scotland there is no body responsible for the independent scrunity of police misconduct.

Inspectorial bodies appointed by the Secretary of State and accountable to Ministers monitor the conditions found in prisons. In Northern Ireland an additional non-statutory adviser monitors conditions in the RUC Holding Centres used for the detention of terrorist suspects and reports to the Secretary of State. His role, again, is limited to giving advice to the Government.

There are no independent arrangements established for monitoring the conditions under which children and young people are detained in custodial care nor any body which can receive and investigate complaints from them, except where the complaint comes within the definition of maladministration in which case the matter could be considered by the local ombudsman - the Commissioner for Local Administration.

Public administration Commissions: The Ombudsmen

Where standards of public administration in Government or the public sector fall below acceptable levels an individual's human rights may be prejudiced, particularly where the conduct of public officials is motivated by bias, unfair discrimination or other prejudice. Throughout the UK, ombudsmen have been appointed with powers and legal responsibility to receive and investigate complaints of maladministration in Whitehall, the NHS and local government.[40] In Northern Ireland the Commissioner for Complaints has specific responsibility for investigating complaints of religious and political discrimination by public authorities and has the power, uniquely within the UK, to apply to the County Court to have his or her recommendations enforced by mandatory order.

Privacy and information rights

Human rights include the right to privacy and to obtain access to one's own personal information held by others. The Council of Europe Convention on Data Protection led to legal protection in the UK for the privacy and accuracy of personal data which has been automatically processed. Data users must register with the Data Protection Registrar (DPR) and comply with a body of principles and regulations. Non-registration or non-compliance with these requirements may lead to prosecution or a complaint to the DPR which may result in proceedings before the Data Protection Tribunal.

The Registrar is constituted as a corporation sole, is a Crown appointment and reports directly to Parliament. The role of the Registrar's office is multi-functional with complaints investigation and registration forming only part of its activities. In addition, her staff promote responsible use of personal data by public authorities and commercial users; feed views into the development of national policy which has a privacy dimension, and promote public awareness of the rights and responsibilities under the Act.

An EU Directive on Data Protection required the UK Government to introduce new rights and protections into the law by October 1998, extending the scope of the Act to include all information, however processed. A Bill to implement the Directive began its passage through Parliament in February 1998.

For other aspects of privacy, only inadequate common law protections are currently available.[41] The Press Complaints Commission is a non-statutory body set up in 1991 and funded by the newspaper industry to receive and investigate complaints from the public about the conduct of the newspaper and periodical industry. Although it has a number of independent members it is essentially a private self-regulatory body, applying an administrative Code of Practice framed by the industry itself.

Article 8 of the ECHR will, through the Human Rights Act, provide a statutory right to privacy for the first time on which case law will be developed by the courts.

Non-governmental organisations

Independent organisations with a mandate to promote human rights, and those working to protect the interests of a particular social group, may variously provide advice to members of the public who believe that their rights have been infringed; take test cases before domestic courts and to the European Commission and Court of Human Rights in Strasbourg; research issues of public concern, conduct inquiries into matters inadequately addressed by official bodies; brief Parliamentarians on the implications of proposed and existing legislation and policy; and seek to promote a better public understanding of rights and the responsibilities they entail.

The contribution which NGOs make to human rights protection will always be of vital importance. Their flexibility and dynamism can rarely be matched by statutory bodies constrained by tighter mandates and accountability procedures. NGOs, however, also operate within constraints and cannot fulfil all of the roles which can be fulfilled by a statutory body:

- Enforcement may require the exercise of legal powers - such as those needed to ensure co-operation with an inquiry - and it would not usually be appropriate to invest a non-public body with such powers.

- Individual NGOs are unlikely ever to have the resources or expertise necessary to provide legal assistance to individuals on the wide range of human rights cases which may arise. Nor can they conduct the range of research, nor engage in the extensive promotion work needed.

- Post incorporation of the ECHR, public bodies will need advice and training on the new standards which they will be expected to meet if they are to avoid challenge in the courts, standards which will change as the law develops. NGOs are unlikely to be accepted by public bodies, such as the immigration or prison service, as their principal source of good practice guidance, even if the NGOs had the resources to provide that service.

- NGOs do not have a duty to be guided in their approach and priorities, by the public interest. They may be constrained, for instance by the sources of their funding, to avoid unpopular or controversial issues which ought to be taken to court.

Parliamentary Human Rights Committee

The Government has suggested that the proposed Parliamentary Human Rights Committee could fulfil at least some of the functions of a Human Rights Commission. We sought views on whether such a Committee would be an adequate substitute. None of those who responded thought that it would. While there is undoubtedly a need for the Committee to strengthen the scrutiny of legislation and policy by elected representatives and to call government to account more effectively, they argued that it should be in addition to, and not a substitute for, a Human Rights Commission. For example, the Commission for Racial Equality:

> The CRE shares the views of others that a Joint Committee of Parliament on its own will not be capable of carrying out the vital tasks needed to create a human rights culture and to enforce ECHR rights. Additional provision is required, which could involve the establishment of an independent body for that purpose, a Human Rights Commission.[42]

The majority of MPs (and Peers, if it were a Committee of both Houses of Parliament) would come from the party in government. Although Select Committees have at times taken a critical view of government policy, they are less likely to do so if the Government is strongly committed to a particular policy and the issue is controversial. The Committee could not be relied upon to take a robustly independent view.

Secondly, most members of the Committee would not have expertise in international human rights law. The expertise which the Clerks to the Committee could provide would not match that which the Committee could receive from an independent Commission with whom it should ideally have a close and complementary relationship.

Third, the Committee would be able to undertake only a small proportion of the roles, described above. It could conduct only a limited number of inquiries and commission limited research from its few staff. It could not undertake a strategic enforcement role, back test cases or initiate proceedings against government or public bodies for failing to meet human rights standards. Nor could it advise individual complainants. It could not undertake promotion and education work nor speak with an independent expert voice to the press and media.

Conclusion

The UK is legally bound by a wide range of international human rights standards, of which a limited number are enforceable in the UK's courts and tribunals. The international enforcement machinery, other than the Strasbourg court, has little impact on UK law and practice: the effectiveness of UK prevention and enforcement mechanisms is therefore essential.

The existing law on one important area of human rights protection, discrimination, is more advanced than in many other areas but is nevertheless patchy and limited. The public bodies that exist to promote and enforce that legislation are hampered by limitations in the law, by lack of resources and by their division into separate organisations. The differences in their mandates and their functions are unhelpful to those needing access to them.

The Data Protection Registrar provides a service in relation to certain aspects of privacy but has no mandate to cover key areas such as wire-tapping or most aspects of press intrusion. There are no public bodies specifically charged with promoting and enforcing the international standards on social, economic and cultural rights. There is no public body concerned with the rights of immigrants and asylum seekers. Although Immigration Act detainees come with the remit of the Prisons Ombudsman, this had not proved an effective remedy.

Incorporation of the ECHR will extend the range of enforceable rights and effectively impose new legal duties on public bodies to uphold them. The existing statutory bodies will not be able to provide any kind of service - advice, monitoring or promotion - in relation to most of the rights which will become enforceable when the Human Rights Act comes into force. They will not be able to provide advice on the right to a fair hearing, for instance, support cases challenging denial of the right to family life, monitor for compliance with freedom of expression or promote awareness of the right to manifest one's religion. If individuals believe that these rights have been infringed, or public bodies want advice on how to avoid doing so, there is no existing public body to which they could turn.

As Baroness Williams argued:

> ..we are looking at a picture of fragmented and in many ways disassociated organisations, each looking after some aspect of

human rights, each one thrust into the picture by the pressures of the constituency that it serves...what we are looking at is an extraordinarily uncoordinated structure of concern for human rights with wide gaps between the organisations which currently exist. Those gaps may in part be filled by the Bill but they will not be satisfactorily filled if there is no provision for a human rights commissioner or commission. There is no overarching theme. There is no common culture of freedom to be found in this picture.[43]

In Northern Ireland the proposed Human Rights Commission could remedy the weaknesses of the existing SACHR, to the extent that it is given a sufficiently broad mandate, adequate powers and resources. In Chapter 4 we assess the extent to which the Northern Ireland Bill does make provision for an effective Commission.

In many jurisdictions abroad, the need to ensure that rights are enforceable in practice, and that adequate steps are taken to avoid human rights infringements, have been met by establishing a 'national institution for the protection and promotion of human rights'. The next chapter looks at the experience of those bodies and at the motivation of the United Nations, Council of Europe and the Commonwealth in promoting their establishment and effectiveness.

Endnotes

1   Under the Race Relations Act 1976, the Sex Discrimination Act 1976 and the Disability Discrimination Act 1995.

2   Such as those in the UK discriminated against due to their age or, in Great Britain, their religious or political belief.

3.   For a comprehensive treatment of many relevant treaties, see Klug F, Starmer K and Weir S (1996) *The Three Pillars of Liberty: Political Rights and Freedoms in the United Kingdom* Routledge; Wallace R (1997) *International Human Rights: Text and Materials*, Sweet & Maxwell.

4.   For a complete list of all UK cases heard by the European Court of Human Rights between 1966, and June 1996, see *Human Rights Legislation* (1996), The Constitution Unit.

5.   *Silver and others -v- United Kingdom*, ECHR Series 'A', No.61 (25 March 1983); *Campbell & Fell -v- United Kingdom*, A 80 paras. 60-63

(1984); *Weeks -v- United Kingdom* ECHR Series 'A' No.114 (2 March 1987); *Thynne, Wilson and Gunnell -v- United Kingdom* ECHR Series 'A' No.190 (25 October 1990).

6. *X -v- United Kingdom* A 46 (1981).

7. *Dudgeon -v- United Kingdom* ECHR Series 'A', No.45 (22 October 1981).

8. *O and H -v- United Kingdom* ECHR Series 'A', No.120 (8 July 1987); W, B *and R -v- United Kingdom* ECHR Series 'A', No.121 (8 July 1987).

9. *The Sunday Times -v- United Kingdom* ECHR Series 'A', No.30 (26 April 1979); *Goodwin -v- United Kingdom* 27 March 1996 (16/1994/463/544).

10. *Boner -v- United Kingdom* A 300-B. paras. 41-44 (1994); *Maxwell -v- United Kingdom* A 300-C paras. 38-41 (1994).

11. Children's Rights Development Unit (1994) UK *Agenda for Children.*

12. For example, Equal Pay Act 1970, Race Relations Act 1976, Sex Discrimination Act 1976, Data Protection Act 1984, Disability Discrimination Act 1995, Access to Health Records Act 1989, Children Act 1989.

13. See Lord Lester of Herne Hill, 'Discrimination: What can Lawyers learn from History?' 1994 *Public Law* 224.

14. Klug F and Starmer K (1995) *The Battered Shield: the system for protecting human rights in the UK*, The Democratic Audit of the UK, Essex University Human Rights Centre; Klug F *et al* (1996) *op. cit.*. For an analysis of the implications of the ECHR for UK mental health legislation see Thorold O 'The Implications of the European Convention on Human Rights for United Kingdom Mental Health Legislation' [1996] 6 EHRLR 619-636.

15. A separate IPPR report by Bynoe I and Cooper J, *Human Rights in Whitehall and Westminster*, deals with this subject and is due to be published in 1998.

16. Kinley D (1993) *The European Convention on Human Rights: Compliance without Incorporation* Dartmouth.

17. Written Answer, House of Lords 15 October 1996 Co. WA 185. Cabinet Office (1992) *Questions of Procedure for Ministers* Cabinet Office, paragraph 8.

18. The Government's proposals for future legislation and policies on Employment Equality in Northern Ireland. Cm 3890.

19. See forthcoming report by Cooper and Bynoe, *op cit.*

20. *Bringing Rights Home: Labour's plans to incorporate the European Convention on Human Rights into UK law, A consultation paper.* December 1996; *Rights Brought Home: the Human Rights Bill*, CM 3782, October 1997.

21. s. 20 1973 Act gave SACHR two purposes, the second of which was repealed by the Fair Employment (Northern Ireland) Act 1976:

    (a) advising the Secretary of State on the adequacy and effectiveness of the law for the time being in force in preventing discrimination on the ground of religious belief or political opinion and in providing redress for persons aggrieved by discrimination on either ground.

    (b) keeping the Secretary of State informed as to the extent to which the persons, authorities and bodies......[public authorities] have prevented discrimination on either ground by persons or bodies not prohibited from discriminating by that law.

22. Its costs for 1994 amounted to £258,900.

23. See Standing Advisory Commission on Human Rights (1987) *Religious and Political Discrimination and Equality of Opportunity in Northern Ireland, Report on Fair Employment*, Cm 237 HMSO; Fair Employment Act 1989.

24. HMSO Cm 3684, June 1997.

25. For example, into incidents of public disorder associated with sectarian marching. See Submission by the Standing Advisory Commission on Human Rights to the Independent Review of Parades and Marches, October 1996, SACHR.

26. Standing Advisory Commission on Human Rights (1990) *Religious and Political Discrimination and Equality of Opportunity in Northern Ireland, Second Report*, Cm 1107 HMSO Paragraph 10.4.

27. Bradley A, Finnie W and Himsworth C (1987) *Discrimination on Religious and Political Grounds: A report for the Standing Advisory Commission on Human Rights in Northern Ireland*, SACHR.

28. See Standing Advisory Commission on Human Rights (1990) *op.cit.*, paragraph 10.10

29. see its *Submission to the UN Committee against Torture*, October 1995 and *Submission to the UN's Human Rights Committee*, July 1995.

30. Sex Discrimination Act 1975, s.59; Race Relations Act 1976, s.50.

31. See Lord Lester of Herne Hill, QC 'Discrimination: what can lawyers

learn from histort?' (1994) *Public Law* 224-237, *op cit.*

32. Ewing K (ed.) (1996) *Working Life: A new perspective on Labour Law* Institute of Employment Rights/Lawrence & Wishart.

33. Morris A and Mott S (1991) *Working Women and the Law: Equality and Discrimination in Theory and Practice* Routledge; McCrudden C (1987) 'The Commission for Racial Equality: Formal Investigations in the Shadow of Judicial Review', chapter in Baldwin R and McCrudden C (eds) *Regulation and Public Law* Weidenfeld and Nicholson.

34. *Amin v Entry Clearance Officer, Bombay* [1983] 2 AC 818.

35. *Perera v Civil Service Commission* [1983] IRLR 166

36. Commission for Racial Equality (1985) *First Review of the Race Relations Act 1976*; and see also CRE Annual Report 1993-4 p.18 (1992) *Second Review of the Rac Relations Act 1976.*

37. Commission for Racial Equality Second Review of the Race Relations Act 1976: A Consultative Paper. John Whitmore. Undated.

38. Discrimination Law Association response to IPPR consultation paper, April 1997.

39. Hepple, Lester, Ellis, Rose and Singh (1997) *Improving Equality law: the Options,* Justice and Runnymede Trust.

40. Parliamentary Commissioner for Administration (GB); Northern Ireland Parliamentary Commissioner for Administration; Health Service Commissioners for England and Wales, and Scotland; Commissions for Local Administration in England, in Scotland and in Wales; Northern Ireland Commissioner for Complaints.

41. Eady D (1996) *op.cit.*

42. CRE response to IPPR proposals, July 1997

43. Committee Stage, Human Rights Bill, HL, 24 November 1997, col 842-3

3. The International Experience[1]

In this chapter we give a brief survey of the growing movement to establish national human rights institutions throughout the world and reveal some of the lessons to be learned from overseas experience. We focus on the UN's *Paris Principles* which established guidelines for these bodies and demonstrate some of the ways in which those principles have been implemented.

Global development

The rapid growth in the number of national human rights institutions is one of the most significant developments in the protection of human rights since the war. Although the oldest Human Rights Commissions date from the 1970s, they have been most enthusiastically promoted and assisted by the United Nations since 1991. The Commonwealth Secretariat has similarly encouraged this development, many of the oldest national institutions being those within Commonwealth countries (Australia, New Zealand and Canada) as well as some of the most recent (India, South Africa, and Sri Lanka).

Francophone Africa has also seen development towards Commissions, as in Cameroon, Togo and Benin. In Europe, Latvia was the first of the new democracies in the former Soviet bloc countries to set up a Human Rights Office. In Ireland the official Constitution Review Group recommended in 1996 that a Commission be established and the Irish government is now committed, by the Good Friday Agreement, to establishing one. Countries which are in the process of establishing Commissions include Papua New Guinea, Mongolia, Nepal, Bangladesh and Thailand.

The growing support for the establishment of these institutions reflects a recognition of the limits to what can be achieved by the international human rights machinery created after the Second World War and by domestic courts:

> International human rights machinery is extremely weak and seldom effective or binding. Such international mechanisms are slow to react to global changes whereas national institutions can respond to specific situations more quickly and effectively[2]

The protection of human rights is primarily a national responsibility. This is made clear in the international human rights instruments which require States not only to respect rights but to take appropriate measures to ensure that those rights are protected. During the 1990s, the development of effective national institutions has come to be seen as one key mechanism to achieve that objective.

The Paris Principles

For the last two decades the United Nations has, through the Office of the High Commissioner for Human Rights, taken an active role in promoting the establishment of national human rights bodies. At its instigation, the first International Workshop on National Institutions was held in Paris in 1991. It formulated a set of principles, endorsed by the UN General Assembly in 1993, covering the mandate and independence of such bodies. The decision to do so reflected, in part, a concern that the credibility and authority of all national institutions could be undermined if some bodies were established which lacked the independence and powers to be effective.

The Paris Principles[3] have since become the yardstick against which national human rights institutions are measured, a base-line standard which leaves considerable scope for each State to determine the most appropriate kind of institution for that country. The Principles state that the mandate, composition and role of the national institution should be established by the State's Constitution or by statute. Its mandate should be as broad as possible and its responsibilities include the right, acting on its own initiative or by request to submit opinions, proposals, reports and recommendations to Parliament, government and other competent authorities on any human rights issue, including any violation of human rights, and to publicise its opinions.

It should be able to examine existing and proposed legislation for conformity to fundamental human rights principles, to recommend new legislation and new administrative measures, and to hear any person and obtain any information and any documents necessary for assessing situations within its competence. It should also be able to contribute to programmes for research and teaching about human rights and to promote awareness, particularly through the press and media.

The national institution should be composed of people broadly representative of those involved in the protection and promotion of human rights, have adequate funding and its own staff and premises, in order to be independent of the Government and not be subject to financial control which might affect that independence.

The full text of the Paris Principles is reproduced in Appendix 1.

Further developments through the UN

In 1993 the World Conference on Human Rights at Vienna endorsed the 'important and constructive role played by national institutions for the promotion and protection of human rights'[4] and encouraged the establishment of such bodies in those countries which had not yet done so.

Significantly, on that occasion national institutions were granted separate speaking rights from their governments. The UN is currently considering whether to formalise this arrangement to enable those national institutions which conform to the Paris Principles to address the Commission on Human Rights in their own right.[5] In 1995 the UN Centre for Human Rights published a comprehensive Handbook providing guidance on establishing and strengthening national institutions and the Centre gives practical assistance to States which decide to do so. The UN hosts the Co-ordinating Committee of National Institutions, currently chaired by the Indian Commission.

The Council of Europe has also been promoting the establishment of human rights institutions in European countries. Under its auspices three meetings of national institutions have been held since 1994[6] and the Committee of Ministers has recently adopted recommendations encouraging member states to establish them. (See Appendix 2)

Breadth of mandate

The Paris Principles sought to define national institutions as having as broad a mandate as possible and the UN Handbook argues that the breadth and depth of an organisation's mandate is a good indication of the value of its role:

> A national institution with a narrow, carefully circumscribed mandate and little independent authority may lack the knowledge, experience and will to advise widely. Conversely, an institution with a broad mandate and independent status will, by definition, possess a grater capacity to acquire and

> synthesise information and, thereby, to develop sophisticated
> opinions on human rights matters for transmission to those
> able to effect substantial change.[7]

Nevertheless, bodies which cover only discrimination issues, such as
the Human Rights Commission in Canada, are described as national
human rights institutions. This is not the case if they cover only one
discrimination issue, such as race or gender.

Ombudsmen, in contrast, usually have jurisdiction to ensure fairness
and legality in public administration and their principal focus is on
complaints of maladministration. Some ombudsmen, however, have a
promotional role similar to that of a Commission, or can investigate
human rights violations, as in Zimbabwe. This chapter deals with the
work of national human rights institutions rather than the often related
work of ombudsmen.

Structure

Varying models of Commission have developed according to the
existing pattern of institutions, to whether the country is a unitary or
federal state and to the breadth of the mandate they are given. In some
countries, Human Rights Commissions coexist with specialised
commissions. In size they vary from small institutions to the 70 member
National Advisory Commission on Human Rights in France.

In Australia, the development of its Human Rights and Equal
Opportunity Commission occurred in stages. The first Human Rights
Commission was set up in 1981, prior to the appointment of separate
Sex and Race Discrimination Commissioners (although a separate
Commissioner for Community Relations had existed since 1975). In
1986 an expanded Human Rights and Equal Opportunity Commission
opened its doors and, in the subsequent five years, the separate
Commissioners on race and sex discrimination were absorbed into the
national commission. A Privacy Commissioner was appointed in 1989.

Rather than establish a single unitary structure the government had
chosen to set up an 'umbrella' model whereby each of the constituent
parts retained its essential identity and its Commissioner became part of
the larger institution. Successive Australian Human Rights
Commissioners, Brian Burdekin and Chris Sidoti, have consistently
argued that there are a number of advantages in having an integrated

body rather than separate bodies dealing with different grounds of discrimination and other aspects of human rights.

One advantage is pragmatic. When the Australian government wished to demonstrate that the rights of a particular community, or a particular human rights issue, required greater attention and resources, it was able to appoint an additional Commissioner rather than establish additional, separate Commissions. Thus in 1993, the Aboriginal and Torres Strait Islander Social Justice Commissioner was appointed and a Disability Discrimination Commissioner in 1992. The former appointment has had a significant impact on the terms of the public debate about the return of land taken from Aborigines - now debated not as a land rights issue but as a matter of human rights. The fact that the Commissioners have different powers with respect to their own jurisdictions has, Sidoti argues, not presented any operational difficulty.[8] Budget cuts in 1997 (to around A $12 million) led to a proposal that there be a reduction in the number of Commissioners and that the office of the Privacy Commissioner, which has never been as fully integrated, separate from the Commission. Under the proposals the President would become the ultimate authority in the Commission which has 130 staff, reduced from 240 by the budget cut.

In New Zealand the Human Rights Commission, established in 1978, has six Commissioners and a broad jurisdiction including discrimination on the basis of employment status as well as on the basis of sexual orientation, family status and religion. Its budget (1996-7) is NZ $4-5 million. The Commission includes a Privacy Commissioner and a Race Relations Conciliator who has his own staff. There is also an entirely separate Children's Commissioner and a Health and Disability Services Commissioner.

A former New Zealand Chief Commissioner addressed the concern that some issues might be swamped within a general Commission and not given sufficient priority. She argued that this can be dealt with by giving particular responsibilities to identified sections of the organisation and ensuring that they are adequately resourced; or by creating separate offices linked under one umbrella organisation.[9]

The mandates of the federal and provincial Human Rights Commissions in Canada (with the exception of Quebec) are restricted to dealing with discrimination issues defined in statute, albeit a broad range - the federal Commission deals with discrimination on the grounds of sex, race, colour, national origin, religion, age, disability, marital status, family status, physical or mental disability and pardoned criminal conviction. Individuals seeking remedies for other fundamental human rights must go to court, whereas discrimination complaints can be investigated by the Commissions without charge to the individual. The federal Commission has generalist Commissioners who, in practice, specialise in different areas of discrimination. Its budget (1997) is C $15.5m.

South Africa's recently established Human Rights Commission (1995), which has constitutional status, has a mandate which encompasses all fundamental human rights, but a separate Commission was established to monitor, investigate, research, educate, lobby, advise and report on issues concerning gender equality. There are also separate Commissions covering linguistic and cultural minorities and youth. The Human Rights Commission has around ten full or part-time Commissioners who take responsibility for particular issues and for particular areas of the country. They meet bi-monthly to make key decisions, for instance on litigation. Its chief executive is accountable to the full time chairman of the Commission. Staff deal with individual Commissioners on a day to day basis. The Commission has committees on specific issues to draw in experts from academia and NGOs. The difficulties caused by the proliferation of Commissions, and shortage of resources, have led to proposals for constitutional amendments to create a single Commission.

The USA has no national human rights commission. Its Employment Opportunity Commission conducts investigations of discrimination in private and federal government employment and promotes voluntary compliance with the statutes through a variety of educational and technical assistance programmes. The Commission on Civil Rights covers discrimination on the grounds of race, colour, religion, sex, age, handicap or national origin. It has no enforcement role but undertakes research, evaluates federal laws and the effectiveness of government equal opportunity programmes and serves as a clearing house for civil rights information.

International human rights standards: the yardstick

The terms of reference of many but not all of the Commissions are defined with reference to international human rights instruments. In some cases the Commission's statute refers specifically to those instruments binding on the State concerned. The Latvian Human Rights Office has a duty to promote observance of fundamental rights and freedoms in accordance with '...international human rights treaties which are binding on Latvia...'. In Australia specific international instruments are listed in the Commission's statute, including the International Covenant on Civil and Political Rights, the Conventions on the Rights of the Child, on the Elimination of Racial Discrimination, and on the Elimination of Discrimination Against Women, and the Declarations on the Rights of Mentally Retarded Persons and on the Rights of Disabled Persons. In contrast, the Guatemalan and New Zealand statutes refer to the international instruments in general. The mandate of the Canadian Commission, however, refers to no international standards but to the Canadian Human Rights Act.

The advantage of relying on the international standards is that it provides a benchmark against which the Commission can measure the legislation or administrative practice that it is examining. It compares those measures to standards which the State has promised to uphold and, by doing so, may secure reforms which prevent later censure by the international bodies which supervise compliance with those standards.

In 1996, the Latvian Human Rights Office compared Latvia's treatment of non-citizens with international standards and concluded that, while it was legitimate to exclude non-citizens from voting rights, it was not acceptable to ban them from a wide range of employment, including that of fire-fighter and licence holder for a veterinary pharmacy. Similarly it reported that, while the legislation providing protection for disabled people was compatible with the relevant international standards, it was not effectively enforced and made recommendations accordingly.

The Danish Centre for Human Rights compared the law and practice in relation to the elderly, the mentally ill and children to Denmark's international human rights obligations. The reports were submitted to the relevant Ministers, Parliamentary Committees and the public. The key issues were deprivation of liberty of the elderly, the right to privacy of the mentally ill and the right of children to have two parents. In all three areas, legislation is now being changed and practices revised in order to implement international standards.[10]

Margaret Mulgan, from her experience as Chief Commissioner of the

New Zealand Human Rights Commission, argued that:

> it is, in my view, highly desirable that such a link (with the UN human rights instruments) exists and that the jurisdiction of the national institution be clearly recognised as exercised within that context. It is that link which makes explicit the role of a national institution for the promotion and protection of human rights, by giving some content to the 'human rights' mandate and by establishing the institution's primary role as overseeing the implementation by universal standards.[11]

National human rights institutions are one effective means of protecting and promoting international economic and social rights standards which are regarded as less suitable for judicial determination. India, New Zealand and Australia are among those which have done so. The Australian Commission conducted an inquiry into homelessness and its effects on young people, relying on the (then) Declaration of the Rights of the Child and the ICCPR as the yardstick against which it measured the adequacy of housing provision. The Indian Commission has, for example, focused on the problem of child labour and has undertaken a project to prevent congenital mental disabilities resulting from malnutrition. The South African Committee has a statutory duty to monitor the implementation of socio-economic rights, such as access to housing, and requires each government department to submit periodic reports on their progress. It can subpoena Ministers to ensure that their departments comply.

Independence

In the *Paris Principles* the prerequisite of an acceptable and effective Commission is its independence. It is crucial that those public bodies which monitor the exercise of power by the State and its agencies should be able to operate as freely as possible from government control. This is the basis of the requirements that institutions be able to act on their own initiative, that they have an appointment process which ensures political independence and prevents arbitrary dismissal, that they have their own staff and premises and financial arrangements which do not deter them from taking controversial decisions.

The UN Handbook notes that independence is a relative concept:

> Independent legal status should be of a level sufficient to permit

an institution to perform its functions without interference or obstruction from any branch of government or any public or private entity.[12]

The French National Consultative Commission on Human Rights is considered influential but may be thought not to fully comply with the independence requirements of the Paris Principles because it is based within the Prime Minister's office and its members are chosen by the Prime Minister. Its membership includes representatives of 28 national associations, 6 trade unions and 21 representatives of religious denominations and academics. It is an advisory and promotion body and has no complaints nor enforcement function. It has, however, had the power since 1989 to act on its own initiative and express opinions contrary to those of the government. A member of the Commission has described it as:

> an entirely novel, unprecedented meeting place for representatives of the state, voluntary sector and civil society who have learned to work together and understand each other better in an extremely frank, sometimes lively, atmosphere, but always with positive results.[13]

Acting on own initiative

The Paris Principles make clear that Commissions should have the power to initiate an investigation without referral from higher authority or receipt of an individual complaint. This is the case in most Commissions. The right to act without referral does not prevent a Commission from being asked to take action. The Indian Commission was asked by the Supreme Court in 1996 to investigate a series of cremations that took place in the Punjab of allegedly unidentified bodies, and agreed to do so.

Financial independence

The Paris Principles stress the importance of financial arrangements which preclude political interference. The UN Handbook advises that funds should *not* be linked to the budget of a government department. In New Zealand, the Commission's funding is channelled through the Ministry of Justice, an arrangement which has caused concern, as has the same arrangement for the South African Commission. The Latvian

Human Rights Office has had reason to be concerned about the need to insulate its budget from political disputes about its role. In 1995 the office was allocated 97,000 lats from the national budget but had this sum cut to 14,272 lats by Parliament, only to be rescued by an allocation of 25, 476 lats from the Cabinet's reserve fund. In 1996, some members of the Parliament proposed cutting the budget so severely that the Office staff would have to be reduced from 17 to 6, but were unsuccessful. On a separate occasion, however, the Office was fiercely attacked by a Government Minister because of its criticism of proposed legislation on Citizenship. On that occasion, the Office survived because of Parliament's support.[14]

The Canadian Federal Human Rights Commission reports directly to Parliament and its budget (of around C $15 million) is allocated by the treasury, not from within any department's budget. Some of the provincial Commissions, however, are more integrated within the structure of the provincial governments. The Australian Commission had its budget cut by over 40 per cent for the three-year period from July 1996, following a change of government.[15]

Appointments

A system for appointing Commissioners, which provides neither government nor parliament with full control, has proved of central importance in guaranteeing the independence of national institutions. The UN Handbook advises that the founding statute should set out the terms and conditions applicable to their appointment and dismissal including the criteria, method and duration of appointment, the permissibility of reappointment, who may dismiss Commissioners and for what reasons, and Commissioners' privileges and immunities. The institution's membership should be broadly representative of society.

The members of the Indian Commission are appointed for a fixed term by the President of the Republic, their names having been recommended by a committee which includes both the Prime Minister and the Leaders of the Opposition in both Houses of Parliament. The Director of the Latvian Human Rights Office is appointed by the Cabinet of Ministers and approved by the Parliament for a term of four years. The six Commissioners in New Zealand, on the other hand, are appointed by the Governor-General on the recommendation of the Minister of Justice for a fixed term (five years), and report annually through the Minister to Parliament. The Australian Human Rights Commission, and the President of the Commission, are appointed by the Governor-General.

The human rights institutions in Uganda, Tanzania and Benin are all composed of direct presidential nominees. In Uganda, the appointment must be approved by Parliament. 17 members of the board of Belgium's Centre for Equal Opportunities and Racial Equality (established 1996) are appointed by Prime Ministerial decree and the remaining 7 by local and regional authorities. In Zimbabwe and Zambia, the presidential power of appointment is exercised on the recommendation of the Judicial Services Commission.[16] In Spain, the Defender of the People (established 1978), whose role is to defend fundamental rights and to monitor the government's activities, is elected by a (three-fifths) majority of the Congress and Senate.

The Commonwealth Secretariat notes that:

> whatever the appointment process, the crucial requirements for appointees is that they are demonstrably politically neutral and persons of high integrity and standing. Without these characteristics, the office is unlikely to gain the confidence of the public.[17]

Impartiality

Commissions have to exercise care to be seen to be independent of political parties. The New Zealand Commission came under criticism during the general election campaign in September 1996 for declaring that some of the policies of one political party, the Christian Coalition, were discriminatory and would breach the Human Rights Act.[18] The Australian Commission does not directly advise the Opposition parties, only providing them with material which has been made public. It will not comment on policy during an election period except to the extent that it will correct factually incorrect information. The Canadian Commission noted in its 1995 Annual Report:

> The Commission has no place in the political arena, on the right or the left, and it should not confuse itself with lobby groups which have their own purpose.

Accountability

An important corollary of independence is that the body should be fully accountable for its activities. The UN advises that accountability must be a two-way process - to government or parliament on the one hand, and to 'the constituency it was established to assist and protect' on the other.[19] Legal and financial accountability are fulfilled through reporting requirements, in some cases to a government Minister and in others by reporting to a Parliamentary Committee.

In New Zealand, a memorandum of understanding between the Commission and the Minister of Justice was agreed in 1996 to clarify their relationship. It dealt with the provision of information and reports by the Commission to the Minister, consultation on budget requirements, quarterly meetings, responses to Parliamentary questions and those from international bodies, assistance to Cabinet Committees, appointment of new Commissioners, and consultation on proposals to change the Commission's statutory responsibilities.

In Australia and New Zealand, the Commissions report to Parliament *through* the Minister. In New Zealand the report is discussed on the floor of the House and by the Justice and Legal Affairs Committee. The Commission also reports regularly to Parliament's Health Committee. The South African Commission submits quarterly reports to the President and to the National Assembly on serious issues which have been investigated, and may submit additional reports at any time. It bears no accountability to the Government, although the Minister of Justice answers Parliamentary questions about its work.

In relation to accountability to the public, the UN Handbook stresses transparency and ensuring that the Commissions' reports are widely disseminated. Commissions should set themselves a policy goal of high visibility and devise a strategy to achieve that goal, a strategy in which the media can be a valuable partner.

It is also suggested that Commissions should evaluate their own performance and make the outcome public. To do this, they need to identify the criteria by which their own effectiveness can be regularly measured. In that way they can adopt the most effective strategies and adapt to changing circumstances and opportunities. A poll initiated by the Latvian Human Rights Office to assess awareness of its existence and identify which issues concerned the public, was one useful initiative of this kind. Another is recording the number of the organisation's recommendations which have been implemented and test cases which have led to changes in the law. The Australian Commission commissioned a review of its complaints handling function in 1993; most of the review's recommendations were implemented.

Functions of Human Rights Commissions

The Australian Human Rights and Equal Opportunity Commission is an example of a body with a wide range of functions. In addition to the statutory responsibilities of its discrimination Commissioners to investigate and conciliate complaints, and of its Aboriginal and Torres Strait Islander Social Justice Commissioner, the functions of the Commission are:

- to examine enactments and proposed legislation to ascertain whether they are contrary to any human right and report its conclusions to the Minister (Attorney General);

- to inquire into any act or practice which may be inconsistent with any human right. The inquiry need not be initiated by a complaint. If appropriate, to attempt by conciliation to effect a settlement of the matters which give rise to the inquiry; or to report on its findings to the Minister;

- to promote an understanding and acceptance, and the public discussion of, human rights;

- on its own initiative, or when requested by the Minister, to report to the Minister on the action which it believes needs to be taken by Australia to comply with the provisions of key international instruments;

- to publish guidelines for the avoidance of practices which are inconsistent with human rights standards;

- to intervene in court proceedings that involve human rights issues;

- to do anything incidental or conducive to the performance of any of these functions.[20]

Scrutinising and drafting legislation

One of the most exacting roles for national institutions is the scrutiny of existing and proposed legislation. Their role is different from that performed by government officials. It is not to assist governments to implement their chosen policies but to advise on the compatibility of those policies with the state's international human rights commitments and with human rights standards. In making that judgement, a Commission brings to the task its experience of dealing with the practical implications of legislation through its advice, complaints and inquiry functions.

The Indian Human Rights Commission drafted a Bill to replace India's 1894 Prison Act, and conducted a review of the Terrorist and Disruptive Activities (Prevention) Act 1987 which led it to recommend in 1995 that the law should not be renewed. The recommendation was accepted. The French Commission has, in recent years, scrutinised Bills concerning bio-medical ethics, the dissemination of racist ideas and the control of migration.[21] The Australian Commission worked closely with the government in drafting its 1992 Disability Discrimination Act. The South African Commission is similarly advising government on drafting equality legislation.

The New Zealand Commission has a statutory responsibility to report to the Government by 31 December 1998 on whether any existing Act, regulation, government policy or administrative practice is incompatible with the 1993 Human Rights Act. The Government has, however, given notice of repealing this requirement. The Commission may also recommend new legislation and successfully argued for an extension of its own mandate in the 1993 Act to include, *inter alia,* discrimination on the grounds of disability (which includes HIV status).

The scrutiny role is one which can bring national institutions into conflict with their respective governments, as in 1991 when the Australian Commission argued, unsuccessfully, that proposed legislation to ban all advertising containing 'political matter' would be an infringement of freedom of expression. In the draft Bill, 'political matter' was very widely defined and 'advertising' was not defined at all. Subsequently, the High Court of Australia ruled that the legislation breached an implied right of free speech in the Australian federal Constitution and was therefore invalid.[22] The Australian Commission is regularly asked for its opinion on draft legislation, although never apparently by the immigration department. In 1994 it advised that some provisions of the Tasmanian Criminal Code breached the ICCPR by prohibiting all forms of sexual intercourse between men, provisions that were also the subject of a critical report from the UN's Human Rights Committee.

The Canadian Federal Human Rights Commission, having argued unsuccessfully for amendments to its legislation to enable it to deal more effectively with discrimination against homosexuals, finally achieved legislative reform in June 1998.[23]

Investigation and Inquiries

When an issue ranges wider than an individual complaint, many Commissions find the power to hold inquiries to be one of their most effective mechanisms to draw attention to the need for reform. Inquiries can be used to investigate a range of human rights issues, identify structural problems, generate valuable research, recommend detailed solutions, educate the public and, to a limited extent, empower sections of the community who are marginalised.[24]

The broad power in the New Zealand Human Rights Act 1993 provides the necessary mandate:

s5(1)(g) To inquire generally into any matter, including any enactment or law, or any practice or any procedure, whether governmental or non-governmental, if it appears to the Commission that human rights are, or may be, infringed thereby;

Public hearings are a means to draw both the public and voluntary and professional groups into the debate and to engender public support for the recommendations made. Inquiries by the Australian Commission have included the treatment of the mentally ill, racist violence and discrimination in the provision of health services to an Aboriginal community. The Commission has the power to enter premises to obtain information and to subpoena witnesses. All of the Australian States have changed their mental health legislation as a result of the Commission's inquiry recommendations. In the course of its inquiry into homeless children it conducted hearings in 21 centres across the country and heard evidence from over 300 witnesses. Advertisements in newspapers invited written submissions and elicited more than 160. The inquiry commissioned studies and visited 20 refuges and youth centres. The report was presented to the Government 18 months after the inquiry began. As a result, most state Governments implemented a major programme of reforms, for which the federal Government provided Aust. $100 million (over four years). In 1997 the Australian Commission presented to Parliament its inquiry report on the *Removal of Aboriginal and Torres Strait Islander Children from their Families*. The Government rejected its central recommendation that the children were entitled to compensation but allocated almost A $30 million to implement many of its other proposals.

Inquiries are not always into controversial issues. In 1994, the Canadian Federal Commission investigated the accessibility of automated banking machines to people with disabilities and recommended design improvements. A second investigation found that more than 25 per cent of the federal government departments and agencies did not provide information in Braille, large print, computer diskette or audio cassette and made recommendations accordingly.

The Indian Human Rights Commission has considerable powers when carrying out investigations to compel the production of evidence and can propose the prosecution of individuals. This is necessary because the cases it investigates include allegations of rapes and deaths in custody, torture in interrogation and collusion between police and kidnappers. Its annual reports cite many cases where its recommendations have been accepted. The South African Commission similarly has the power to subpoena witnesses, take out search warrants and hear evidence when investigating human rights violations.

Enforcement

A key distinction can be drawn between those bodies which are purely advisory, and those which can take enforcement action if they believe human rights standards have been infringed or if recommendations, following an investigation or the adjudication of a complaint, are rejected. The French Commission is an example of a purely advisory body. It believes that any enforcement role would, being confrontational, be incompatible with its existing relationship with the Government. The Mexican Human Rights Commission can similarly only make recommendations even after it has investigated a complaint. The Mexican Government believes this to be effective:

The strength of its recommendations is of a moral nature, in accordance with the Commission's credibility in society, and is enhanced by the fact that failure to comply with its recommendations will be commented on in its periodic public reports, which would imply a high political cost for the authority involved.[25]

Others do not share this sanguine view of the Commission's effectiveness The National Commission, and its state counterparts:

have been largely ineffective in reducing or sanctioning human rights violations primarily because they are powerless to prosecute violators or create the institutional accountability needed throughout the Mexican government to inhibit violations. Furthermore, virtually endemic violations of labour rights and electoral rights remain outside the Commissions' mandate.[26]

In 1992, less than 39 per cent of the Mexican Commission's total of 412 recommendations were fully implemented by government agencies. Between 1990 and 1994 over 300 people were killed under circumstances related to electoral disputes and irregularities, but the Commission was not able to investigate any of the underlying allegations of voting rights violations.[27] This criticism underlines the insistence in the *Paris Principles* that such bodies should have a broad, inclusive, mandate.

Advice is of no value if it is entirely ignored. The UN advises governments to establish in the founding legislation clear channels within government and Parliament 'for acquiring, channelling and utilising the advice' to ensure that the national institutions receive a considered response. It advises the institutions to monitor the outcome of each recommendation and to publish it.[28]

Advice will not always be accepted even by governments which are generally receptive. The Chief Commissioner in New Zealand noted in 1993 that the Commission's advice had been accepted in relation to corporal punishment in schools, the reintroduction of the death penalty and the treatment of mental health patients, but not on the treatment of refugees under emergency procedures instituted during the Gulf War.[29] More recently, advice on legislation requiring assets to be sold to pay for long term health care led to those provisions being repealed. The Australian Commission was successful when it recommended that the Australian Defence Force's ban on homosexuals should be removed.

Investigation and adjudication of complaints

Many Commissions have a responsibility to examine individual complaints. Some Commission refer complaints to the appropriate investigative authority or institute legal proceedings itself. This is the case in New Zealand. Some Commissions have a responsibility to conciliate between the complainant and the body against which the complaint is made. They operate a range of different kinds of alternative dispute resolution mechanisms which can form a compulsory first stage before access to the courts or adjudication by the Commission.

The New Zealand Commission has the power to investigate complaints about a broad range of discrimination issues. If the complaint has substance it adopts a variety of means to effect a conciliation, including round-table meetings and negotiations by telephone, fax and letter. In these negotiations it is impartial. The Commission cannot itself impose a settlement but it has the power to call a compulsory conciliation conference between the parties and, if a settlement is reached, it is legally binding. Settlements can include apologies, assurances against repeating the behaviour, compensation, reinstatement, transfers, access to services previously denied, implementation of new policies and references. In 1993-4, 49 per cent of the complaints dealt with by the Commission concerned sex discrimination, 12 per cent disability, 10 per cent age, and 4 per cent both race and religious belief. The majority of complaints related to employment (58 per cent). If unsuccessful in conciliation, the complainant or the Commission can take the complaint to a Complaints Review Tribunal which makes a ruling and can award compensation.

The Australian Commission, which receives about 1500 complaints a year, has the power to adjudicate allegations of discrimination, as is the case in Canada. Most complaints are conciliated or withdrawn, rather than proceed to the next stage which, in Australia, is a formal determination by the Commission sitting as a Tribunal. The Commissioner who was involved in attempts at conciliation does not sit as a member of the Tribunal. The Commission believes that its attempts at conciliation are frequently effective precisely because there are enforceable remedies if conciliation is not successful.

In relation to other kinds of complaints, for instance on the rights of children, the Australian Commission does not have the power to adjudicate and can only make recommendations to Parliament, a procedure which it considers to be an unsatisfactory way of dealing with individual cases. 10 - 15 per cent of the Commission's resources are allocated to complaint handling. Its current Human Rights Commissioner argues that the investigation of complaints is one important means by which the organisation gains credibility. It can speak from experience of the problems to which particular legislation or administrative practices can give rise.

The Commission in Canada can dismiss the complaint, appoint a conciliator or send the complaint to the Human Rights Tribunal for a binding decision. An appeal can be lodged with a review tribunal or the courts.

The new South African Commission has also been given responsibility for investigating and conciliating complaints and receives around 200 each week. The case for this approach is that the Commission can provide remedies that are realistically accessible to the majority of the population who could not afford to use the courts. It offers scope for conciliation which can have wider implications than just resolving the problem for the individual concerned, such as redesigning the policy which led to discrimination. Approaching the Commission is also cheaper for individuals than using the courts. If conciliation fails, however, its recommendations have to go before a court for enforcement.

Some Commissions, for instance those in Canada and Australia, can accept discrimination complaints on behalf not only of one individual but also a group or class of people similarly affected. This is seen to have advantages: it may be impractical to deal with a large number of individual cases together and multiple complaints, if dealt with separately, could lead to inconsistent results. It also helps to ensure that a general problem is not dealt with as the problem of one individual. A class action was taken in Australia under the Disability Discrimination Act 1992 challenging Telecom's refusal to provide TTY machines for profoundly deaf subscribers. The Commission, sitting as a Tribunal, found against Telecom, requiring it to make TTY available at no cost to over 20,000 people.

In some cases complaints can be lodged by third parties, for instance if the individual is in detention, severely disabled or very young. Uganda, Toga and Namibia are among those Commissions which will investigate complaints submitted by national or international NGOs. The Australian legislation specifically provides those in detention with the right to contact the Human Rights Commissioner without interference by the authorities.[30] Restrictions preventing detained asylum seekers from taking advantage of this right were challenged by the Human Rights Commissioner in court in 1996, a challenge which was successful.

The kinds of individual complaints dealt with by Commissions vary widely in different parts of the world but many issues recur. Latvia's Human Rights Office has many complaints about conditions in detention, the behaviour of the police, decisions by the Department of Immigration and Citizenship and about the difficulties of finding work. The Indonesian Commission (established 1994) has received many complaints about land claims and labour rights, on which it can make recommendations but not binding determinations.[31] In the 12 months to April 1998, the Indian Commission received 38,000 complaints.

Litigation

Where Commissions do not have determination powers they may support complainants in taking their case to court. The Australian Commission cannot represent an individual in court but is instrumental in their receiving legal aid. Many Commissions can also institute court proceedings on their own behalf.

Some Commissions may also, with the leave of the court, intervene in legal proceedings to bring relevant principles of international law to the attention of the court. A former Australian Human Rights Commissioner has argued that this function can be 'of considerable relevance both in its direct effect in individual cases and in educating the judiciary and the legal profession generally'.[32] That Commission has used its power of intervention to great effect. In the *Teoh* case for instance[33] the High Court accepted its argument that ratification by the Australian government of a human rights treaty created a legitimate expectation that the executive government would act in accordance with the treaty provisions. An immigration officer should, therefore, have taken into account the Convention on the Rights of the Child in deciding whether to deport from Australia a father of seven children. The House of Lords in a previous English case had reached the opposite decision on this principle.[34] The South African Commission has also intervened in a number of cases at the request of the President of the Constitutional Court.

Promoting awareness and training

Most Commissions provide training to some of those responsible for upholding human rights standards: government officials, the police, armed forces and employers are among those either receiving training or being provided with assistance in developing their own training programmes. The South African Commission, for instance, has conducted workshops at the invitation of government departments, including that responsible for immigration. It also trains the trainers, working with them to produce training manuals. They often draw on the expertise of individuals outside of the Commission to help in producing material.

National institutions invariably have a duty to promote awareness of human rights principles and do so by varying means and with variable success. The Latvian Human Rights Office produced 10,000 leaflets in Latvian and Russian to inform people about their rights. The Office is working with teachers to prepare new material for primary schools and has circulated a brochure on family violence. It has also had its own TV slot, *'The individual and his/her rights'*.

The New Zealand Commission, with a duty 'to promote, by education and publicity, respect for and observance of human rights', includes within its library 60 video-tapes covering a range of human rights issues. Reflecting its emphasis on discrimination, it holds seminars for employers and service providers, and publishes a wide range of information sheets on the Human Rights Act and on specific aspects of discrimination. Of the 6,458 enquiries it received for information during the year 1993-4, 13 per cent concerned age discrimination, 9 per cent sexual harassment, 8 per cent work disputes, and 8 per cent disability.[35] It has been able to establish a self-funding sexual harassment prevention consultancy because of the level of demand for its training services.

The Canadian Federal Commission responded to more than 600 enquiries from journalists in 1995 and put out several public service announcements on radio. These thirty second items used the voices of ordinary Canadians to explain the meaning of human rights in everyday life. It launched an information service on the Internet in the same year. As part of its efforts to raise awareness it published a series of *'Real People'* posters emphasising that many people with disabilities lead ordinary active lives.

The Australian Commission has a library which is open to the public with on-line and CD Rom data base searches available. It ran a major publicity campaign to raise the awareness of women about the protection provided by the Sex Discrimination Act against sexual harassment, focusing on prevention.

The French Commission publishes an annual report on racism and xenophobia which includes a poll of public opinion and a report on government measures. It has an on-line database of case law about racism with the complete text of judgements in national courts going back more than 20 years. It awards an annual prize for contributions to human rights protection and promotion.

The Indian Commission has adopted a threefold strategy to fulfil its responsibility to 'spread human rights literacy'. It solicited the support of the leadership of each of the political parties and made specific suggestions about how *they* could promote human rights, monitor the conduct of their cadres and keep in contact with the Commission. It approached the Chief Minister of each State with specific ideas on the training and sensitising of their officials, and made suggestions to the education authorities and to universities on how human rights could be included within the curriculum, including reviewing textbooks prejudicial to human rights, introducing a source-book of human rights materials and establishing university level courses. The Commission also encourages debate in the media, for instance on the issue of child labour and has used events such as UN Human Rights Day as a focus.[36]

The South African Commission allocated R1m for public education work in 1997. Its work includes assisting the government to develop curricula for human rights education in schools, promoting alternatives to corporal punishment and circulating information and posters on the Bill of Rights – in 11 official languages.[37]

International role

For most of the national institutions, an international role is auxiliary rather than central to their functions. For a minority, such as the

Commissions in Equador and in France, it is more significant. The French Commission has represented the French position in multilateral negotiations on human rights issues and contributes to the preparation of the reports which the French Government submits to the international supervisory bodies. It comments on human rights abuses in other countries and encourages the Government to take appropriate action. It also played a role in bringing together the first conference of national institutions in Paris in 1991 and the first conference of European national institutions in Strasbourg in 1994; and has provided advice and assistance to some of the new African bodies. The advantage of this dual role is the direct connection it fosters between the stance taken on human rights issues abroad and that in domestic policy.

Commissions elsewhere make a contribution which is sometimes more clearly independent of the position taken by their own government, including participating as experts on delegations to UN treaty monitoring bodies. The New Zealand Commission is regularly consulted over the preparation of reports to the Treaty bodies; the Australian Commission was part of the Australian Government delegation negotiating the UN Convention on the Rights of the Child.

Relationship with non-governmental organisations

The UN stresses the importance to Commissions of working with NGOs: the support of NGOs can enhance the visibility of the Commissions by making the public more aware of their existence; NGOs can serve as an intermediary for victims of violations; they can provide detailed information about the situation on the ground and the inadequacies of current legislation; and they can provide a complementary partner in particular projects and educational initiatives.[38]

National institutions work with NGOs in a variety of ways. When the Togo Human Rights Commission was set up in 1987, its membership included two lawyers elected by the Bar Association, a representative of the Red Cross and elected representatives of women, youth, workers and traditional chiefs. The Mexico Commission has a formally constituted advisory body of human rights experts which conducts studies and makes recommendations to the Commission.

The New Zealand Commission has worked with NGOs on the preparation of a mental health report (1991), in a study on housing issues and in its work on prisons and on refugees. Its statute requires it to 'consult and co-operate with other persons and bodies concerned with the protection of human rights'. Australia's Privacy Commissioner has an advisory committee comprised of interested organisations, while the charter of its Human Rights and Equal Opportunity Commission specifically mandates the body to work with NGOs. It took account of NGO views when preparing its recommendations to government on the draft UN Convention on the Rights of the Child and has commissioned reports from NGOs, for instance on the need for increased protection for people with disabilities. It has found NGOs to be vital in encouraging and assisting individuals to give evidence to its inquiries.

Conclusion

The *Paris Principles* took the first step in establishing internationally accepted guidelines for national human rights institutions and the UN Handbook has complemented those principles with detailed guidance. In practice, the mandates, structure, functions and powers of the growing number of institutions differ widely and some more clearly conform to those international standards than others. Little has yet been written on the effectiveness of these young institutions and their own literature is generally more descriptive than evaluative.

Nevertheless it is evident from the number of enquiries received, complaints handled, inquiries conducted, litigation initiated and recommendations accepted that many are fulfilling important and expanding roles. The trend is towards establishing such national institutions in those countries which do not yet have one and to enhance the effectiveness of those institutions already established.

Endnotes

1.   The authors acknowledge with thanks the research conducted by Marie Pool and her first draft of this chapter.

2.   Report of the Commonwealth Workshop on National Human Rights Institutions, Ottawa, Canada, p19. Human Rights Unit, Commonwealth Secretariat.

3.   Principles relating to the status of national institutions for the promotion and protection of human rights, endorsed by the Commission on Human Rights in resolution 1992/54 and by the General Assembly in resolution

48/134 of 20 December 1993.

4. Vienna Declaration and Programme of Action, Part 1, para 36.

5. Report of the Commission on Human Rights Fifty-third session, 9 April 1997, National Institutions for the Promotion and Protection of Human Rights, E/CN.4/1997/L.67.

6. The Second European Meeting of International Institutions for the Promotion and Protection of Human Rights was held in Copenhagen in January 1997. Organised by the Danish Centre for Human Rights in co-operation with the Council of Europe, the Organisation for Security and Co-operation in Europe (OSCE), the UN High Commissioner for Human Rights and the Commissioner of the Council of the Baltic Sea States, it led to the formation of a co-ordinating committee for the European bodies, chaired by the Danish Centre.

7. *National Human Rights Institutions*, A Handbook on the Establishment and Strengthening of National Institutions for the Promotion and Protection of Human Rights, para 185. UN Centre for Human Rights Professional Training Series No.4, June 1995.

8. Conversation with the authors in London, 8 April 1997.

9. Mulgan, M (1993), 'Implementing international human rights norms in the domestic context: the role of a national institution', *Canterbury Law Review* (vol.5).

10. Statement by the Director of the Danish Centre for Human Rights to the 54th Session of the Commission on Human Rights, Geneva, 4 April 1998.

11. Mulgan, M 1993, *ibid*.

12. *National Human Rights Institutions*, (1995) *op cit.*

13. Gouttes, R, in Presentation of European National Institutions, Council of Europe, S:\ecri\copen.96\ecri96.47.

14. Latvian Human Rights Office Background Information issued in 1996; Acting Director Kaija Gertnere speaking at the Second Meeting of European international institutions for the promotion and protection of human rights, Copenhagen, January 1997.

15. Human Rights and Equal Opportunity Commission press release Human Rights Commission budget cut by 40%, 13 May 1997.

16. Carver, R, and Hunt, P, *National Human Rights Institutions in Africa*, African Centre for Human Rights and Democracy Studies, The Gambia, 1991.

17. National Human Rights Institutions Manual, Commonwealth

Secretariat, 1993, p20.

18. WYSIWYG NEWS, 3 September 1996.

19. *National Human Rights Institutions*, 1995, op cit.

20. Human Rights and Equal Opportunity Commission Act 1986, S11.

21. Presentation of European National Institutions, extract from the publication *Ce racisme qui menace l'Europe*, the proceedings of the first European meeting of National Institutions in 1994, circulated at the Second European meeting of National Institutions for the Promotion and Protection of Human Rights, Copenhagen, January 1997. S:\ecri\copen.96\ecri96.47.

22. *Australian Capital Television v Commonwealth* [1992] 177 CLR 106.

23. Canadian Human Rights Commission Annual Report 1995.

24. Hunt, P, *Reclaiming Social Rights, International and Comparative Perspectives*, Dartmouth, 1996, p195.

25. UN Doc.E/CN.4/1991/23/Add.1 par 2, quoted in Burdekin, B *op cit.*

26. Sanchez, R, 'Mexico's Governmental Human Rights Commissions: an ineffective response to widespread human rights violations' in *St Mary's Law Journal* (1994) 25, 1041.

27. Sanchez, R, ibid p1053.

28. *National Human Rights Institutions,* (1995) *op cit*

29. Mulgan, M, 1993, *Canterbury Law Review, op cit.*

30. Section 20 of the Human Rights and Equal Opportunity Commission Act 1986.

31. Report of the first Asia-Pacific regional workshop of national human rights institutions, Darwin, Australia, 8-10 July 1996, p9.

32. Burdekin, B 1991, *Human Rights Commissions*, paper prepared for the meeting of National Human Rights Institutions convened in Paris, 7-9 October 1991.

33. *Minister for Immigration and Ethnic Affairs v. Teoh* [1995] 69 A.L.J.R. 423.

34. *R. v Secretary of State for the Home Department*, ex p.Brind [1991] AC 696.

35. Report of the Human Rights Commission and the Office of the Race Relations Conciliator for the year ended 30 June 1994.

36. National Human Rights Commission Annual Report 1994-5.

37. Dr.Pityana addressing a British Council conference in Belfast, May 1998.

38. *National Human Rights Institutions,* (1995) *op cit*, para 108.

4. Functions and Powers

This chapter considers what the Human Rights Commissions in Northern Ireland and in Britain should do: their roles, functions and powers. For Northern Ireland, many of the proposed functions were set out in the Agreement reached at the multi-party talks on 10 April 1998. The Northern Ireland Bill to establish the Commission was subsequently published on 15 July 1998. We comment on those proposals which, only in part, match our own.

When we use the term Human Rights Commission in this chapter we are referring equally to the proposed Northern Ireland Commission and to a UK Human Rights Commission, unless we specify otherwise. While we advocate that each of those Commissions should have the same basic functions and powers, we recognise that the priorities of the Northern Ireland body would necessarily reflect the differing circumstances in that part of the country.

Good Friday Agreement[1]

The Agreement specified that the remit of the Northern Ireland Human Rights Commission would include the following tasks:

- keeping under review the adequacy and effectiveness of laws and practices, making recommendations to Government as necessary;

- providing information and promoting awareness of human rights;

- considering draft legislation referred to them by the new Assembly;

- in appropriate cases, bringing court proceedings or providing assistance to individuals doing so;

- to consult and advise on the scope for defining, in Westminster legislation, rights supplementary to those in the ECHR, to reflect the particular circumstances of Northern Ireland, drawing on international instruments and experience. These additional rights to reflect the principles of mutual respect for the identity and ethos of both communities and parity of esteem and - taken together with the ECHR - to constitute a Bill of Rights for Northern Ireland.

● to consider the formulation of a general obligation on government and public bodies fully to respect, on the basis of equality of treatment, the identity and ethos of both communities in Northern Ireland and a clear formulation of the rights not to be discriminated against and to equality of opportunity in both the public and private sectors.

We comment on these functions and those set out in the Northern Ireland Bill as we consider the options for the functions of the Commissions in the sections which follow.

Broad mandate

The role of the Human Rights Commission could be defined narrowly in relation solely to the rights in the European Convention (ECHR) and those additional statutory rights which are already enforceable within UK law. Alternatively, its mandate could relate to the UK's broader international human rights obligations such as the UN Convention on the Rights of the Child and the Council of Europe Framework Convention on Minorities. The breadth of its role will determine, in part, the specific functions which the organisation is expected to fulfil.

The Parliamentary debates on a possible UK Commission took place in the context of the Human Rights Bill and therefore necessarily focused on the role of the Commission in relation to the rights in the ECHR. However, the role which the body could play in raising awareness of the UK's wider international obligations was acknowledged. The importance of that role was also firmly endorsed in many of the responses which IPPR received to its consultation paper, not least those from organisations, such as those working with children or with disabled people, for whom the ECHR offers far less than other more recent international Conventions.

The Commission for Racial Equality:

Having regard to the limitations of the ECHR and to the wider framework of rights which are protected under other international instruments, the CRE urges that the promotional and educational work to develop a human rights culture should encompass not only the ECHR but also the other international covenants by which the UK has agreed to be bound which include racial equality as a fundamental right.[2]

In our view it is essential that the Commission's mandate is drawn from the breadth of international human rights law, not confined to the narrow and in many ways limited ECHR. The UN guidelines stress the importance of a broad mandate, not least because of the recognition that the Commission will be weakened and seen to be ineffective if human rights issues of major public concern are repeatedly to be found to be beyond its powers to investigate or provide assistance:

> Actual or potential strength and effectiveness are directly related to the legal mandate of the institution. A national institution which is rendered weak and ineffective by its constitutive law can increase its technical competence, but in the absence of legislative change it will never completely overcome its structural inadequacies.[3]

While the primary focus of the UK Commission's work is likely to be within the remit of the ECHR, it should be able to draw attention to those wider obligations binding on the UK when these provide a more appropriate yardstick against which to measure the standards of public authorities.

The Standing Advisory Commission on Human Rights in Northern Ireland has continually found it necessary to work outside of its narrow statutory remit but has only been able to because of the willingness of the government of the day to allow it to do so. It told IPPR:

> SACHR's experience has shown that a body without a strong statutory remit may have limited authority. While SACHR's limited statutory remit has not prevented the Commission from advising on areas other than those laid down in statute...it is clearly easier for any Secretary of State not to accept the recommendations of a body which, in many key areas of its work, is advising without statutory authority.[4]

The Law Society similarly argued:

> We agree that it is essential that the scope of the Commission should not be limited by the content of a single human rights or anti-discrimination instrument. However, even limiting its area of operation to a number of statutes and instruments could mean large areas of injustice which deserve attention do not receive it ... The new body should be able to direct the attention of government to a wide range of issues where rights are threatened or are under threat of compromise.[5]

The importance of international standards other than the ECHR has been recognised in relation to the Northern Ireland Commission which will be expected to advise the Government on the extent of rights additional to the ECHR which should be incorporated within a Bill of Rights for Northern Ireland. The Northern Ireland Bill defines its mandate in terms of 'human rights'. That term, according to the Bill, *includes* the rights in the ECHR.

Opinions differ on where the emphasis should lie in the work of the Commission. While some stress that its primary function should be that of ensuring access to justice for individuals who believe that their rights have been infringed, and to support or initiate test cases, others stress the educational role which the body should play, raising awareness and promoting good practice. In Northern Ireland, particular importance is attached to provision of the powers necessary to investigate human rights abuses. While the emphasis differs, few have dissented from the range of functions which our consultation paper outlined:

Prevention

- Promoting good practice

- Promoting awareness and education

- Scrutiny of proposed legislation and policy

- Monitoring compliance with the UK's international human rights obligations and advising Government on the effectiveness of the arrangements for protecting human rights

Enforcement

- Providing access to justice
- Initiating and supporting test cases
- Investigation

Prevention

Ministers assume that the Human Rights Act, by imposing an obligation on public bodies to respect the rights in the ECHR, and by giving individuals a right to challenge them if they do not, will itself change attitudes. The Lord Chancellor told the House of Lords that 'a culture of awareness of human rights will develop'[6] but there is no reason to be confident that the change in the law alone will bring about that significant change. Its impact could largely be limited to the outcome of individual court cases. Baroness Williams:

> One of the most important changes that a Human Rights Commission could bring about would be a gradual extension of the culture of human rights ... I fear that what we may see instead is a piece of legislation that comes to be seen as a lawyers' inside world, a world which excludes those who are not lawyers.[7]

The Human Rights Commission should in our view be charged with responsibility to raise awareness of the implications of the Act and of the UK's wider human rights obligations:

- among the *public bodies* (and private bodies exercising public functions) which are bound to comply with the provisions of the European Convention;

- amongst the *general public*, including young people, whom the Government wants to develop a culture of rights and responsibilities;

- within *Whitehall and Parliament*, charged with ensuring that legislation and public policy do not infringe human rights standards.

The Northern Ireland Bill states that the Commission 'shall promote understanding and awareness of the importance of human rights' for which purpose it can undertake research or educational activities.

Promoting good practice within public bodies

Home Office Minister Lord Williams of Mostyn told the House of Lords:

> Every public authority will know that its behaviour, its structures, its conclusions and its executive actions will be subject to this culture. It is exactly the same as what necessarily occurred following the introduction of, for example, race relations legislation and equal opportunities legislation. Every significant body, public or private, thereafter had to ask itself with great seriousness and concern, 'Have we equipped ourselves to meet our legal obligations?' That has caused a ... transformation in certain areas of human rights. The same is likely to follow when this Bill becomes law.[8]

The difference between the Human Rights Act and those earlier pieces of discrimination legislation is that there were two statutory bodies - the EOC and the CRE - to ensure that organisations were aware of their obligations under the law and to encourage them to adopt good practice. Public bodies will equally need to be made aware of their new obligations under the Human Rights Act: how, for instance, they should interpret the requirements of the ECHR that they protect 'private and family life', refrain from 'degrading treatment' or ensure that individuals have access to a 'fair hearing'. If they do not receive guidance on good practice they may lay themselves open to challenge in court.

The existing equality Commissions have sought to find the right balance between promoting good practice by employers and service providers and using the law to challenge discrimination. Where such organisations have been willing to adapt, more has been achieved through training and advice than through litigation.

The Human Rights Commission should similarly seek to promote good practice, particularly within those institutions which have the greatest impact on the civil rights of vulnerable people: the police, prison and immigration service, and institutions for the care of children, and the mentally and physically disabled. The Commission could approach those responsible for these services and institutions, co-operating on Codes of Practice or training manuals, providing advice on how to avoid breaching the Convention, devising procedures which will both protect vulnerable people and protect the institution from challenge in the courts.

The Commission could also promote the standards in those wider human rights Conventions which the Government has undertaken will be met throughout the UK. It could, for instance, advise local education authorities and residential homes on the implications of the UK Convention on the Rights of the Child. As in all of its functions the Commission would need to use its resources strategically, working through the leadership of public bodies, and through other organisations, to reach a wider audience. The experience of some Human Rights Commissions abroad has been that it is more effective to teach the senior officers in organisations such as the police and armed forces how to incorporate human rights principles into their training than to undertake that training themselves.[9] Baroness Williams:

> I believe the training and education of public bodies is just as important as the establishment of case law...I fear that, for failure to train them in what the Bill means, we shall see a great deal of litigation that is unnecessary, expensive, slow, tedious and repetitive.[10]

> It is of the most crucial importance that we prevent what otherwise might be a series of cases reaching the courts, none of which need to do so, simply because we failed to inform those responsible for administration at central government, local government and citizen level about the impact of the Bill.[11]

The judiciary and magistrates will also need to acquire new expertise in handling ECHR issues and £5 million has been set aside by the Government for their instruction.

The Northern Ireland Agreement makes no mention of the Commission's potential role in promoting good practice within public bodies.

Promoting awareness and education

The Human Rights Act requires public bodies to change the way in which they treat individuals, but has less direct implications for the behaviour of private bodies and of individuals. Yet the Lord Chancellor has expressed the hope that it will nevertheless have that broader impact and that the proposed Parliamentary Committee on Human Rights could itself be:

> in the forefront of public education and consultation on human rights. It could receive written submissions and hold public hearings at a number of locations across the country. It could be in the van [sic] of the promotion of a human rights culture across the country.[12]

The Committee could indeed play an important role in raising awareness. But it could not perform the full range of education functions outlined here, any more than existing Select Committees have been able to do in relation to the issues within their remit. Baroness Williams:

> the great advantage of a Human Rights Commission or Commissioner is that it would make human rights open to the public, it would encourage the public to own human rights in a way which would not be exclusive either to Parliament or to the legal profession but should be the beginning of a real and profound change in the democratic ethos and sense of freedom in this country.[13]

Overseas human rights bodies have used a variety of means to increase public awareness. The resources of the UK Commission would be limited, although it might be able to attract private or charitable funds for its promotion and education work or assistance in kind (such as free advertising space). It would need to rely on the least expensive means to get its message across - and act as a catalyst to others to promote its message rather than producing large quantities of expensive materials itself.

The Commissioners could use the press and broadcasting media to ensure that the human rights dimension of public debates is brought to the fore. Often this would not be to assert the over-riding importance of upholding a particular right but to reflect on the balance which needs to be struck between competing rights or between a human right and conflicting social policy objectives. In relation to CCTV, for instance, the Commission might draw attention to the need to find the right balance between protecting privacy and the need to prevent crime, and suggest safeguards which would protect that balance. It might comment on the implications of international rights standards for the resolution of a policy dilemma, such as the implications of 'the right to found a family' for policy on in-vitro fertilisation.

This approach would raise the profile of the Commission and public awareness of the significance of human rights principles to everyday life. But it is an approach which would have to be used with care to ensure that the Commission's authority was enhanced and its political impartiality assured. Among many other skills, Commissioners would therefore need to have sound political judgement and be adept in media interviews.

The Commission could find public inquiries a particularly effective means to attract media attention. The Australian Human Rights and Equal Opportunity Commission estimates that the coverage of its inquiry report on the children of Aboriginal parents who were removed from their homes was equivalent to millions of dollars of advertising space and considerably more effective in raising public awareness.

Education

The Government is committed to ensuring that children are taught the principles of citizenship and democracy more effectively than within the current curriculum. It established an advisory committee to advise on how this might be done. Its interim report, in March 1998, did not recognise the role of human rights principles in citizenship education but its final report is expected to address that omission.

The principles in the Convention - like freedom of speech or the right to respect for privacy - could be taught as a set of common values to which the nation subscribes, even if we may differ on the means to achieve them. In the same way that it is now commonplace for children to discuss 'saving the environment' as an accepted common good, despite the fact that views differ widely on how that goal should be achieved, human rights principles should be an integral part of each child's school life.

A recent survey illustrates the extent of ignorance in the UK about human rights standards. Children aged 14-16 in Northern Ireland and in three developing countries were asked, *inter alia,* whether they had been told in school about the rights in the UN Convention on the Rights of the Child. Of the children in Botswana, 43.5 per cent said that they had been told. 68 per cent of children in India and 53 per cent of the children in Zimbabwe said the same. In Northern Ireland, it was only 6 per cent.[14]

The Human Rights Commission could take the initiative to address this ignorance and foster a cultural shift, promoting teaching materials which enable children to discuss the significance of each human right and its protection in law. Is free speech an absolute right and, if not, why not? In what circumstances is it legitimate for the Government, or a parent or teacher, to restrict what an individual can say? If I infringe your right to privacy, can you infringe mine?

Through such discussions, children would gain an understanding of rights, and the responsibilities they entail, which they could apply not only to their daily lives but to their growing understanding of world events. The Human Rights Commission would not necessarily be involved in the production of teaching materials itself, but support the efforts of others to bring human rights education in from the margins to the centre of the education debate.

The Northern Ireland Agreement makes no mention of any role for the Commission in relation to human rights education for children.

Scrutiny

An important prevention role for the Commission would be to monitor the conformity of proposed legislation to the international human rights standards binding on the UK, in particular the ECHR. The Commission would need to adopt a selective and strategic approach to this task, focusing on the draft legislation and policy with the greatest potential implications for human rights. Its function would be to advise the Government and Parliament of any potential breaches of international standards, and particularly of the ECHR, prior to the draft legislation becoming law or an administrative practice implemented. It would be for the Government and Parliament to decide how to respond.

The justification for giving priority to this role is that prevention is better than cure - and cheaper. The record of UK cases before the European Court of Human Rights shows that on a number of occasions government has proposed, and Parliament has accepted, legislation which was later held to be in breach of the European Convention. It is not always possible to say with certainty whether a particular provision will be held to be a breach. But it is also true that some of those cases could have been avoided had government and Parliament given greater priority to ensuring that legislation conformed to the Convention. The inadequacy of current scrutiny procedures is explained in Chapter 2.

The Immigration Law Practitioners' Association:

> The role of the Commission as we see it would be first and foremost to preview legislation and policy proposals and advise Parliament and the government on their conformity with international human rights standards. In our opinion, before legislation is passed and indeed before it is even laid both the government and Parliament should have a full assessment of the human rights consequences of that legislation prepared by a Commission with independence and standing and whose advice is public.[15]

The Commission could also advise on existing legislation and policy, making its own recommendations for reform, or assisting a Select Committee inquiry. It would take care to ensure that its advice on draft legislation or policy was in the public domain to avoid any suggestion that it was providing assistance selectively. It should not comment on the proposals of political parties.

Whitehall officials already scrutinise draft legislation for conformity to the European Convention. When the Convention is incorporated into domestic law, greater priority will be given to this procedure, as the risk of challenge in the courts will be an immediate one. Moreover, the Human Rights Act will require Ministers to inform Parliament whether each new Bill conforms to the provisions of the Convention or not.

This requirement will focus the minds of politicians and civil servants on the potential human rights implications of a Bill. However, the legal advice Government receives will remain private, providing no guidance to MPs and Peers in their debates on the proposed measures. Parliamentarians are currently at a considerable disadvantage when seeking to challenge proposed legislation for conformity to international law. The Minister, when introducing an Immigration Bill, for instance, can reassure MPs that he has been advised that the measure does not breach the right to family life protected by the ECHR, without disclosing the details of that advice. Only those Parliamentarians with expert knowledge of international human rights law could challenge that assurance effectively.

A Human Rights Commission would provide Parliamentarians, not least those on the proposed Human Rights Committee, with the expert advice which would enable them to discuss the implications of proposed measures with greater authority. The Commission could, for example, inform them of the view taken by the European and domestic courts of similar measures and of the factors which judges would take into account should the measure ever be challenged in court.

The Director of Liberty:

> The Commission could assist the Committee by submitting reports and expert advice, providing some sort of balance against the resources available to the executive who are very likely to want to influence the committee in one particular direction.[16]

The Commission, in contrast, would be free from party political considerations, looking to international human rights standards for guidance on the view it should take.

Parliamentarians in Scotland will have no less a need for expert advice as they consider draft legislation under their new powers. The Scotland Bill makes specific provision for draft legislation to be scrutinised for conformity to the Convention and subsequently to be overridden by the Courts if it does not. A Scottish Human Rights Commissioner would give Members of the Parliament direct access to expertise on international standards, and their applicability to domestic law and policy, which is unlikely to be available to them from any other source.

In recommending this role for the Commission, we are not suggesting that it would replace the role of officials. To the extent that the Strasbourg proofing system is enhanced, and the outcome of that process made available to Parliamentarians, the need for the Commission to fulfil this role may be diminished. Equally, if the proposed Westminster Parliament's Committee on Human Rights is well resourced, with staff of sufficient expertise, there may be less need for the Commission to focus on this aspect of its work.

We have doubts, however, that this will prove to be the case. The Government's legal advice will necessarily remain private. There are already concerns whether it will be possible to provide adequate resources for the Human Rights Committee, and the role of a Parliamentary Committee will always differ from that of an independent Commission.

The Good Friday Agreement stated that the Northern Ireland Commission will be able to 'consider draft legislation referred to them by the new Assembly'. The Northern Ireland Bill requires that a copy of each Bill is sent to the Commission (Clause 11). The Commission should also have the power to scrutinise draft Westminster legislation which could equally have significant human rights implications for Northern Ireland.

Monitoring compliance of existing law, policy and practice

Labour's pre-election consultation paper on incorporation of the Convention, *Bringing Rights Home*, gave as one of the potential roles of a Commission the need to monitor the operation of the Act and to ensure the conformity of EU law (and, presumably of UK law itself) with the UK's human rights obligations under international treaties.

The Commission could approach this responsibility in two ways. When looking at an issue causing public concern, for instance the treatment of children in residential care, its report could indicate, *inter alia,* where the practices of the public bodies concerned fell short of the requirements of the European Convention and of wider international standards. Alternatively, the Commission could approach the question from the other direction, taking the standards in a particular Convention and evaluating the extent to which those standards are met by the bodies to which they apply. It might take this approach, for instance, if intending to submit a report to the United Nations supervisory committee responsible for monitoring the implementation of that Convention. In each case, the Commission would advise the Government and the Parliamentary Human Rights Committee of the steps which needed to be taken to ensure compliance with the UK's obligations.

We suggest that, in this context, one of the Commission's statutory responsibilities should be to monitor the adequacy and effectiveness of the arrangements for protecting human rights in the United Kingdom. It should keep under review the existing machinery for promoting and enforcing human rights and advise the Government on whether any legislative or policy reform was needed in order to provide greater protection for the rights of any particular group of people, for instance the elderly, or any particular right, such as freedom of the press.

The Royal National Institute for Deaf People suggested to us that the Commission should, within this role, advise on the content of a future UK Bill of Rights.[17] The Runnymede Trust asked whether the Commission could consider the ways in which protection could be provided for Muslims against discrimination on religious grounds.[18] The Immigration Law Practitioners' Association suggested that it might look at issues such as the exercise of extra statutory discretion by immigration officers or the lack of a presumption in favour of bail in immigration cases (in the context of the right to freedom from arbitrary detention).[19]

Within this remit, we have suggested that the Commission, or a Human Rights Commissioner, could play a key role in advising the Government, after a period of consultation, on the most effective relationship between a Human Rights Commissioner and the existing statutory bodies in the human rights field.

The Northern Ireland Commission will be required to 'keep under review the adequacy and effectiveness of law and practice, relating to the protection of human rights' (Clause 55).

Enforcement

The Human Rights Act will provide individuals with redress, and in some cases with compensation, through the existing courts and tribunals. It is not suggested that the Human Rights Commission should itself adjudicate complaints nor provide redress. Its role should not be to replace court adjudication but to complement it in three ways:

- by enhancing *access* to justice, assisting the public in obtaining expert legal advice;

- by supporting or itself initiating test cases or by submitting *amicus* briefs to assist the court; to encourage the rational and coherent development of a human rights jurisprudence; and

- by *investigating* major incidents or systematic abuse and making recommendations to the government or public authority concerned.

Professor Michael Banton, Chair of the UN Committee on the Elimination of Racial Discrimination:

> The most important objective for a Human Rights Commission is enforcement. Everything else is subsidiary. Enforcement is itself the best promotion.[20]

The Northern Ireland Bill provides for the Northern Ireland Commission to give assistance to individuals in taking cases under the Human Rights Act (only) but not itself to initiate court proceedings.

Access to justice

The Human Rights Act will provide individuals with many new grounds for challenging their treatment by public bodies. Whether the new rights will be enforceable in practice will depend on:

- whether individuals have access to legal advisers who have the necessary *expertise* in what may be fast developing areas of law

- whether they can *afford* to pay for that advice and take the financial risk of going to court

Lord Goodhart:

> If there is no Human Rights Commission or Human Rights Commissioner, what is to happen to the lay person who believes that his or her Convention rights have been breached? They can go to their local Citizens' Advice Bureau but are unlikely to find anybody there who is sufficiently specialised to be able to give sensible advice. They may go to their local law centre, in the unlikely event that they can find one that operates in their area. They may go to a solicitor, but that will cost money for a totally uncertain future...
>
> It would be an enormous help if such a person could go to the Human Rights Commission or Commissioner for advice as to

their Convention rights...for support in bringing the case before the court or tribunal which can give relief.[21]

Master of the Rolls, Lord Woolf, when asked by the BBC whether he foresaw the need for a Human Rights Commission, replied:

> I would give that proposal very sympathetic consideration, speaking personally, I think that one can see in areas where we've had commissions of that sort, after a hesitant beginning they have made a contribution and they are also able to make a contribution in relation to something to which I attach great importance, and that is access to the courts. It is no use having rights if people can't use them.[22]

Lord Lester, noting that incorporation of the Convention introduces new legal hurdles for individuals to overcome before they have exhausted their domestic remedies and can appeal to Strasbourg, argued that individuals must not be deterred by the absence of legal aid or advice, nor by the risks of having to pay the legal costs of the other side:

> The key question here is whether the Government are to provide...the means to enable effective access to justice to be provided and whether there is to be an expert body able to marshal the arguments and the evidence and have authority before the courts in enabling test cases to be properly mounted and argued.[23]
>
> That operates as an extremely important filter. It helps the courts to know that cases that are brought before them are well focused, that they have been through the rigorous screening process, as happens for example with the Legal Committee of the Equal Opportunities Commission.[24]

The kinds of cases which could be raised under the Human Rights Act, whether in new proceedings or allied to other claims or defences are enormously varied. They extend from the strip-searching of prisoners, the unregulated seclusion of psychiatric patients or racial discrimination amounting to degrading treatment, to challenges to family separations caused by care proceedings or immigration control, to surveillance methods used by the police or to restrictions on the freedom to march or to speak about conditions at work.

The Human Rights Act thus has implications for lawyers working not in one field but throughout public and private law. The legal profession will need to advise and act in relation to a new field of unfamiliar law affecting a vast range of possible situations. Its members will need to consider the possibility of new proceedings and new lines of claim or defence. Lay advice bodies (such as Citizens Advice Bureau) will also need to advise the public and to assist them in finding expert assistance and representation. Such bodies are expressing concern that, in the absence of a Commission to which they can refer cases, they may not be able to cope. The 1990 Trust, an organisation which advises black groups and individuals:

> We are concerned that we will be inundated with queries about the Act but unable to provide answers or direct individuals to a central body which will be able to assist.[25]

The Commission could provide advice to individuals, whether directly by telephone or letter. The protection of human rights laws can be most needed by those who occupy the economic, political and cultural margins of society. Often lacking money, personal freedom, social acceptance or strong supporters, such people would find it hard to gain access to the resources of the Commission and benefit from its advisory service unless positive steps such as free-phone lines, outreach visits or targeted publicity, were taken to promote access to the body. Information would need to be available in formats appropriate for those with reading or hearing disabilities. In the case of deaf people this would mean providing appropriate communication support to enable them to communicate with the Commission's staff.

The Commission's informal filtering or screening role would help to ensure that cases which were groundless were quickly identified and that those with merit were handled by competent and cost effective practitioners. This should reduce the chances that weak or hopeless litigation is funded through legal aid at public expense.

In some cases the Commission would refer people to an appropriate source of expertise elsewhere, drawing on the register it would maintain of legal advisers with expertise on particular issues. An important role for the Commission could thus be to act as a referral body, linking people with a network of lawyers in private practice, in law centres and in NGOs who have expertise in human rights law and practice.

We considered the possibility that the Commission might have a role in deciding which cases should receive legal aid. Liberty raised the procedural difficulty that it would not always be clear which cases were primarily raising a human rights issue and therefore be subject to scrutiny by the Commission. The Law Society argued:

> We would not support a further barrier being placed in the way of those needing financial assistance to bring a case concerning infringement of human rights...

However, it suggested that there could be concerns about a lack of expertise or appreciation of human rights issues in legal aid committees and that consideration might therefore be given:

> to devising a procedure so that the new Commission could certify that a case should be granted legal aid which would facilitate its grant through the normal procedure.[26]

British Irish Rights Watch was firmly against any Commission role in relation to legal aid:

> ...it is fatal to the impartiality of what is basically a body offering advice and influence if it becomes the gatekeeper of scarce resources. Those who administer legal aid will have to undergo a learning curve about the merits of ECHR cases, but the appeal system is there to assist in that process and lawyers will have to use it if necessary...
>
> To become the holder of the purse strings would, we think, infringe the principle of independence from government.[27]

Litigation

The Commission could select those cases to which it wanted to offer support or to act in court. It could most effectively select those cases which would test or clarify the law, implementing a test case strategy. For instance, the Commission might support:

- cases under Article 8 involving personal privacy to establish the boundaries of the privacy rights found in the Convention and the extent to which they are circumscribed by rights to freedom of expression

- cases involving standards of detention or punishment in order to limit practices such as the shackling of prisoners receiving medical treatment or when giving birth; the failure to transfer a mentally ill patient to a specialist psychiatric hospital; or the use of medical treatment - such as tranquilliser medication - for non-medical purposes.

- A 'whistleblower's' claim that their right to disclose information in the public interest derives from their Article 10 right to freedom of expression, displacing their employer or professional body's legal power to dismiss or expel them.

Lord Simon of Glaisdale, argued that one of the many advantages would be in weeding out at an early stage some of the hopeless cases as well as bringing success to some of the stronger ones. Baroness Lockwood, the first chairman of the Equal Opportunities Commission, stressed the important role that body had played in this respect and the importance of a Human Rights Commission playing the same role:

> I am very conscious of the important role which that body (the EOC) had in a number of ways in helping individuals to establish their own rights under the law; equally and perhaps even more importantly, testing the various sections of the Act so that potential applicants under the Act would be more aware of their own position and of what were their rights; and just as importantly, in ensuring that those who might inadvertently or advertently contravene the Act would be made aware of the consequences of doing so. In other words, the Commission helped codify the Act by carefully selecting key cases to support and thereby establishing very important case law which was used widely both by individuals and organisations.[28]

The principles in the European Convention are stated in general terms and difficult to interpret across a wide range of varied situations. They need to be applied over a series of cases for relevant rights and duties to become clearly established. Existing caselaw under the Convention will not necessarily offer a reliable guide to its meaning and impact for UK domestic law. This is because judges will only be required to take the jurisprudence of the European Court of Human Rights into account. They could consider that a higher standard is required than has been established in Strasbourg caselaw.

Human rights law thus needs a degree of judicial attention before its impact can be fully appreciated and laws, practices and institutions adapted to it. For this reason, during the early years following incorporation of the ECHR in particular, the UK will need a body which is able to focus on the Convention and help it to realise its full potential. Only a Commission, with powers to participate fully in the judicial system and bring to it selected and significant cases, would be in a position to do this.

Human rights cases, moreover, require expert and extensive preparation enabling the court to receive and consider relevant social data, some of this being obtained from research. Were the Commission to adopt a strategic approach to test cases, it would find itself well-placed to obtain and use such information from its own research work.

Occasionally there might be no litigant able or willing to lend their name to an action. Legal proceedings are costly and can be protracted. They are conducted in the public domain, with sensitive or controversial cases attracting considerable publicity and huge anxiety for litigants. Such factors can strongly discourage individuals from taking proceedings and can influence the stage at which they will be prepared to settle their claim. Furthermore, the scope and outcome of legal proceedings depend upon the particular facts of the case which may not be the ideal grounds on which to test or clarify the law. Finally, individuals, in choosing to pursue their case, are not usually motivated by any concern for the rational development of a body of coherent human rights principles relevant to contemporary social needs. People naturally want justice for themselves and may fear raising risky legal arguments that can be necessary if the law is to develop.

Lord Woolf, Master of the Rolls:

> ...often the infringement is not such that an individual would want personally to get involved in all the complexity and expense involved in legal proceedings. And if there is somebody like a commission or, as I've said in things I've written, equivalent to a Director of Civil Proceedings who people can take their suggested infringement to, and who would then

> consider whether it's something in relation to which the Director
> or Commissioner should bring proceedings, then that would be
> of great benefit to the public.[29]

In these circumstances, proceedings may need to be brought not by an
individual person assisted by the Commission but in the name of the
body itself. The Commission would need to be given specific statutory
powers for that purpose.

The Human Rights Act does not allow public bodies (or voluntary
organisations) to take cases in their own name. Persistent attempts were
made during the passage of the Bill through Parliament to remove that
restriction, without success. The Home Secretary, in a letter to IPPR, did
say that the Government would look again at that restriction were a
Human Rights Commission to be established:

> I obviously agree that, if in due course there were to be
> legislation establishing a Commission with the role among
> others of initiating litigation in its own right, the legislation
> would need to re-visit Clause 7 of the current Bill .[30]

The Government has not, however, done so in relation to the Northern
Ireland Commission, the draft legislation for which does not allow it to
initiate litigation in its own name.

Baroness Amos stressed the importance of a Commission having
this power:

> I recall during my years at the Equal Opportunities
> Commission the importance of the Commission having
> standing to take a case. This will be particularly important
> during the early stages of incorporation, when there will be a
> need to clarify the law. A case brought by a group can clarify
> the law for many people, some of whom may not even know
> of their rights. A well focused case, brought in good time,
> may also save public money - for example multiple legal aid
> costs. In most cases there clearly will be a victim; but I believe
> it is important that we do not now go backwards and limit the
> access to the courts of public interest organisations .[31]

Lord Simon of Glaisdale stressed the financial advantages of this
proposal:

> If we had a Commission for Human Rights and permitted it,
> at the discretion of the court, to have locus standi in these
> matters, part of the denial of legal aid would be solved.
> American courts give that type of *locus standi*. I can see no
> reason why we should not.[32]

and the Law Society argued:

> ...nothing should restrict its ability to bring cases - as the
> existing Commissions may now do - which may extend or
> clarify the existing law.[33]

There are other circumstances in which the Commission could be
involved in court proceedings. Following its own approach or the
court's own initiative, it could be invited by a court to act as *amicus
curiae* to put before the court factual or legal material that would
otherwise not be available to it. This is a practice sometimes used both
in the European Court of Human Rights and in the Canadian Supreme
Court when interpreting the Charter of Rights and Freedoms. In the
Australian courts the Human Rights Commission has frequently
intervened as a full party to the proceedings and its influence has been
felt in changing the law relating to children's rights in particular.

Until the Rules of Procedure operating in the English courts are
amended, the circumstances in which one party can intervene in another
party's action are limited. However, when an appeal reaches the House
of Lords (and with the leave of that court), an intervention can be made.
In recent years Liberty and Justice have each been granted leave to put
an *amicus* brief before the House of Lords in cases involving
interception of telephones and sentencing policy. On occasions, the
Human Rights Commission might wish to intervene at that level and
should have the power to do so.

The Northern Ireland Bill does not specifically provide for the
Commission to intervene in cases but this would not preclude it doing
so.

Service to legal advisers

Finally, the Commission would seek to enhance the ability of other
organisations and legal advisers to provide an expert service. It would
be a source of expertise on which they could draw; a source of material

and a source of training. This service to the legal profession would help to ensure that individuals received appropriate advice and would discourage weak litigation at public expense:

- it could provide training to lawyers and other advisers on human rights law and practice;

- it could facilitate networking among specialist lawyers and other advisers by, for example, holding seminars;

- it could make its expertise available to lawyers and other specialist advisers by publishing Case Digests, or maintaining and publishing on the Internet a database of ECHR cases.

Investigation and public inquiries

The third 'enforcement' arm of the Commission should be the power to investigate major issues of concern - whether a serious incident or a situation appearing to show systematic and persistent human rights abuses. Investigation, where appropriate by a public inquiry, can be a more appropriate means of dealing with such issues than litigation.

Neither the Northern Ireland Agreement nor the Bill include any provision for an investigation or inquiry power (but there is an expectation that this may be remedied by the Government before the Bill is enacted).

The existing equality Commissions have the power to investigate and adjudicate on apparent cases of systematic discrimination. Their investigation is not restricted to specific allegations of illegal activity by identified persons and they have the power to compel the production of evidence so that they can gather sufficient facts to reach a decision on the merits of the allegations. They can then issue a formal non-discrimination notice which requires the organisation to comply with specified changes in practice. In relation to non discrimination issues, such a power to issue binding recommendations might not be appropriate. The Human Rights Commission's investigation could, instead, lead to recommendations to the government or public body concerned.

The experience of Commissions in overseas jurisdictions shows that the use of public inquiries to investigate endemic social problems can be an important tool. Hearing evidence in public around the country can draw considerable media and public attention to the issue, raising its profile on the political agenda. As, unlike an ad hoc commission of inquiry, the organisation continues to exist after the conclusion of the inquiry, it can monitor the implementation of any recommendations which it makes.

The Commission must be equipped with the powers it needs to conduct effective inquiries: a power to subpoena witnesses, to call for the production of documents and to inspect premises relevant to the inquiry's terms of reference. The Paris Principles state that a national institution shall 'hear any person and obtain any information and any documents necessary for assessing situations falling within its competence.' (See Appendix 1). As the Commission may not have within it the necessary expertise or resources to conduct a particular inquiry, it should have the power to appoint temporary Commissioners.

We received strong representations that this role would be a crucial one. The Director of Democratic Dialogue in Northern Ireland:

> In situations where human rights are widely contested (as against where they create individual human rights cases) a broader view needs to be taken of the matters at stake, especially when these escalate to crisis point. In that context, a frequent demand from spokespersons for those who feel in some wider collective sense aggrieved is that an inquiry be held. By definition, such constituencies will feel 'fobbed off' if such an inquiry is internal or otherwise seen as carried out by what they deem the villain of the piece - the powers that be.[34]

Inquiries can help to diffuse the heat from controversy, contribute to building a consensus around areas of broad agreement and ensure that those with competing views at least feel that they have had a fair hearing.

Complaints adjudication

A variant on the court-based model of enforcement is the complaints investigation and adjudication role which is undertaken by bodies such as the Parliamentary Commissioner for Administration (PCA).

For many overseas Human Rights Commissions the investigation and adjudication of complaints is a major part of their role, but usually only in relation to discrimination cases. Some Commissions conciliate between the two parties and may subsequently play a role in the final adjudication of the issue. In contrast to the courts, this system is free to the complainant and resolves the complaint more quickly. Although it has not been proposed that a Human Rights Commission in the UK should investigate and adjudicate complaints, its importance within other Commonwealth Commissions suggests that the case should at least be considered.

There are some strong reasons in favour of the Commission being able to adjudicate individual complaints:

- The Commission is bound to receive many complaints from the public alleging that their human rights have been violated. They may expect the Commission to resolve their complaint;

- Dealing with complaints would help the Commission to keep in touch with public concerns as they arise and give it added authority when voicing its views on current human rights issues.;

- It would provide a cheaper and possibly quicker means for individuals to obtain redress than the conventional judicial system.

We have, however, concluded that the Commission should not be responsible for investigating and ruling itself on such complaints at least initially. There are a number of major objections to it having such a role, which override the advantages.

Providing a complaints investigation, conciliation or adjudication service is highly resource intensive. It could be cheaper than taking cases through the courts but would come from a separate budget and resources would have to be allocated before it was known if long term savings would in practice be made elsewhere.

It is not possible to anticipate what kinds of cases, nor the volume of cases, which will arise under the Convention nor how effectively they will be resolved through the courts. It makes sense to wait and see how adequately existing systems operate before setting up an alternative.

There would be serious disadvantages if the Commission were to combine the role of prosecutor and judge - assisting individuals to take cases through the courts *and* adjudicating complaints internally. The Quebec Human Rights Commission, which once had the power to adjudicate complaints as well as to assist complainants, found those roles to be incompatible in practice and its adjudication role was removed in 1990.

A number of those we consulted drew our attention to the dangers of establishing the body with incompatible functions. For example, the Discrimination Law Association argued that the range or functions allocated to the new body should be carefully considered in order to avoid 'the incompatibilities and internal conflicts' which have marred the current system:

> ...it has proved counter-productive to combine the role of the commissions in assisting litigation and taking enforcement action on behalf of victims with the quasi-judicial role of issuing notices and orders. The latter should be left to courts and tribunals. It is also vital not to combine a law enforcement role on behalf of victims with a conciliatory and promotional role which tends to requires a degree of impartiality.[35]

The Immigration Law Practitioners' Association similarly argued:

> ...we see grave dangers in any contamination of the role of the commission as an investigative body with any role as a dispute resolution mechanism. It is very difficult to reconcile these two functions in a constitutional legal structure based on adversarial principles.[36]

Providing the Commission with adjudicative powers would be likely to lead to a heavy complaints workload and prove highly expensive to finance. This would reduce or eliminate its ability to pursue test case litigation in the courts. The Commission could find itself drawn too closely into resolving a mass of individual disputes, risking its ability to fulfil its wider role.

The Data Protection Registrar shares this view:

> Our experience allows me to endorse the concerns expressed about the balance between public interest enforcement and investigating individual complaints. There is a risk that complaints can distort the priorities and resources given...[37]

For these reasons, we have concluded that the Commission should not be equipped with individual complaints investigation and adjudication powers, nor do we propose the creation of a specialised Human Rights Court or Tribunal to determine individual complaints. Children in

Scotland suggested, as an alternative, that the jurisdiction of the Local Ombudsmen and Parliamentary Commissioners for Administration should be extended to include human rights complaints and that the role of local authority Children's Rights Offices be extended to provide all children with an opportunity for individual redress.[38]

Conciliation

The formal conciliation role played by many Human Rights Commissions abroad arises from their role in adjudicating discrimination cases. We neither propose that the UK Commission should adjudicate human rights cases, nor that a formal conciliation process would be appropriate where an individual's fundamental human rights are at issue. However, there may be many cases where *informal* conciliation by the Commission may help to resolve a situation, and satisfy the complainant, without the issue having to be taken further. A letter from the Commission to the public body concerned, or a telephone call, could result in the decision or practice causing concern being reconsidered. The Commission should have, within its legal department, the resources which would allow it to respond to individual cases in this way, if the complainant wishes that kind of intervention.

Research

Research would not be a function in itself but a means to inform the Commission's monitoring and advice work and its inquiries. Research could be conducted in-house or commissioned from other bodies. For the Commission to speak with authority it would need accurate information and sound analysis. It could develop international research links to be able to draw on comparative material and, over time, provide an invaluable research resource to other organisations in the field.

Were the existing public bodies to become part of the Human Rights Commission, the scope for comprehensive research and data collection would clearly be greater. A database of discrimination cases, for instance, could be compiled and made available to legal practitioners for whom the absence of such a resource is cited as one of the disadvantages of the current fragmented approach to discrimination enforcement.

The Director of Democratic Dialogue, pointing to the influence which research by SACHR has had on the reform of the fair employment legislation, stressed the importance of the Human Rights Commission's research function:

> The trouble with government doing its own research is that it has got too many higher priorities on its agenda, civil servants will always tend to the routine and the safe, and ideologically unwelcome conclusions may be quietly deterred at an early stage or ruled out by the brief.[39]

International role

The UK Commission would assist the UN supervisory bodies in their scrutiny of the UK's record in relation to particular Conventions, for instance the Committee on the Elimination of Racial Discrimination. The Commission would not represent the UK but be present as an independent expert body, a role envisaged by the UN's Paris Principles and already familiar to such bodies as the Data Protection Registrar at a European level. The UN is currently revising its own procedures in order to strengthen the voice of national human rights institutions within its deliberations.

The Minority Rights Group suggested to us that the Human Rights Commission might ensure that the public is better informed about the position which the UK takes at international human rights meetings, and the conclusions which are reached by the supervisory bodies about the UK's compliance with international standards.

While the focus of the Commission would be on human rights within the UK, it could contribute to the promotion of human rights abroad. It could participate in United Nations meetings to promote new international standards, and those of the Council of Europe. Furthermore, it could assist those establishing national human rights bodies in other countries, particularly those within Commonwealth countries where the UK would be a natural source of assistance.

Conclusion

The Human Rights Commission's mandate should be drawn from the breadth of international human rights standards. It should not be limited to the European Convention on Human Rights.

The Commission should fulfil a range of prevention and enforcement functions. It should promote good practice within the public authorities and private bodies covered by the Human Rights Act, and foster a wider awareness of human rights principles amongst the public. It should learn from the extensive experience of Human Rights Commissions abroad in fulfilling these responsibilities effectively.

The Commission should scrutinise draft legislation and policy and advise the Government and Parliament on its conformity to international human rights standards, in particular to the European Convention. Elected representatives at the Scottish Parliament and Northern Ireland Assembly will have no less a need for expert advice as they consider draft legislation under their new powers. All draft legislation should be referred to the Commission. It would be likely to comment only on those provisions with significant human rights implications.

The Commission should also scrutinise existing legislation and policy, monitor implementation of the Human Rights Act, and advise the Government and Parliament on the adequacy and effectiveness of the arrangements for the protection of human rights in the United Kingdom. Within that remit, a Human Rights Commissioner could play a key role in advising, after a period of consultation, on the most effective relationship between his or her office and the existing statutory bodies in the human rights field.

The Commission should not replace enforcement of the Human Rights Act by the courts but contribute to enforcement in three ways: by assisting the public in obtaining access to legal services; by supporting or initiating cases and submitting *amicus* briefs to assist the court; and by investigating major incidents, where appropriate through the establishment of a public inquiry.

The Commission should not be given a responsibility to adjudicate individual complaints. The need for this role could be reconsidered once the effectiveness of the Human Rights Act has been evaluated.

The Commission should undertake research in order to inform its monitoring, scrutiny, advice, litigation and inquiry functions. To speak with authority, it would need accurate information and sound analysis.

Finally, while the focus of the Commissioner's work would be on human rights within the UK, its work would have an international dimension. It could participate in international human rights for a developing new human rights standards or implementation mechanisms. Through the co-ordinating committee of national human rights institutions, it could assist in the establishment of national institutions abroad, as does the Foreign and Commonwealth Office. Most significantly, it could contribute to the scrutiny of the UK's reports to the UN supervisory committees and attend meetings of those committees as an independent expert body.

The proposed Northern Ireland Commission lacks some of these key functions - the power to investigate human rights abuses, to establish public inquiries, to initiate litigation and to scrutinise all draft legislation, not only that from the Northern Ireland Assembly.

Endnotes

1. *The Agreement:* Agreement reached in the multi-party negotiations. 10 April 1998

2. CRE response to IPPR proposals, July 1997

3. *National Human Rights Institutions,* Professional Training Series No.4, 1995, p1, para 2.

4. Response by SACHR to IPPR Consultation Paper, 11 February 1997

5. Response to IPPR proposals from Law Society Employment Law Committee, September 1997.

6. Lord Irvine of Lairg, Second Reading of the Human Rights Bill, HL, 24 November 1997, Hansard col 1228.

7. Committee stage of the Human Rights Bill, HL, 24 November 1997, Hansard col 844.

8. Home Office Minister Lord Williams of Mostyn, Second Reading Human Rights Bill, HL, 3 November 1997, Hansard col 1308.

9. This point was, for instance, made by the representative of the Sri Lankan Human Rights Commission at the IPPR/CHRI conference on Commonwealth national human rights institutions on 16-17 October 1997.

10. Baroness Williams, Committee Stage of the Human Rights Bill, HL, 24 November 1997, Hansard cols 844 and 843.

11. Third reading of the Human Rights Bill, HL, 5 February 1998, col 825.

12. Second Reading, Human Rights Bill, HL, 3 November 1994 col 1234.

13. Committee Stage of the Human Rights Bill, HL, 24 November 1997, Hansard col 845.

14. Richard Bourne *et al*, 1998, *School based understanding of human rights in four countries*. Department for International Development.

15. ILPA Response to IPPR Consultation Paper, 28 February 1997.

16. IPPR Conference, 18 December 1996.

17. Response by RNID to IPPR Consultation Paper, February 1997.

18. Letter from Runnymede Trust in response to IPPR Consultation Paper, 24 February 1997.

19. Response by ILPA to IPPR Consultation Paper, February 1997.

20. Letter from Professor Michael Banton, 19 December 1996.

21. Committee Stage of the Human Rights Bill, HL, 24 November 1997, Hansard col 846.

22. Radio 4, *Analysis*, 6 November 1997.

23. Lord Lester, Committee Stage of the Human Rights Bill, HL, 24 November 1997, col 841.

24. Third Reading of the Human Rights Bill, HL, 5 February 1997, col 821.

25. Paper by the 1990 Trust regarding incorporation of the European Convention on Human Rights and Race Equality, March 1998.

26. Law Society response to IPPR, September 1997.

27. Response to IPPR Consultation 20 May 1997.

28. Committee Stage, HL, 24 November 1997, Hansard col 847.

29. Radio 4, *Analysis*, 6 November 1997.

30. Letter from Rt. Hon. Jack Straw MP to Sarah Spencer dated 17 November 1997.

31. Committee Stage, HL, 24 November 1997, Hansard col 829.

32. Second Reading, HL, 3 November 1997, Hansard col 1260

33. Response from the Law Society, September 1997.

34. Letter from Robin Wilson, 5 February 1997.

35. Comments from Discrimination Law Association on the IPPR Consultation Paper, dated 17 April 1997.

36. Response from ILPA to IPPR consultation paper, 28 February 1997.

37. A Human Rights Commission for the UK – The Options. Appendix 12 to 13th Annual Report of the Data Protection Registrar.

38. 'Proposal for a Human Rights Commission, Implications for Children', April 1997.

39. Letter from Robin Wilson, 5 February 1997.

5. Structure and Accountability

In this chapter we consider the options for the structure of the Commission. We look first at the implications of devolution and advocate a devolved structure with a UK co-ordinating secretariat. Secondly, we turn to the relationship which the Commission might have with those existing statutory bodies which bear some responsibility for promoting and enforcing human rights. We consider the advantages and disadvantages of different models and conclude that the most effective model for the Commission in the long term would not be to operate as a separate body but to bring some existing organisations within its umbrella. Finally, we suggest ways to ensure the accountability of the Commission to Parliament and to the public and consider its relationship with non-governmental organisations. We conclude with an estimate for the cost of the Commission as a separate body in its first year of operation.

National structure: unitary or devolved?

The first question to be resolved is whether there should be separate Commissions, or Commissioners, in Scotland, England and Wales, and what the relationship between the Northern Ireland Human Rights Commission might be with its counterparts in other parts of the United Kingdom.

The UK government is responsible, under international law, for ensuring that international human rights standards are met throughout the United Kingdom. It is held accountable by the European Court of Human Rights and by the United Nations if those standards are breached. The Government must therefore ensure a degree of uniformity in the protection of human rights in all parts of the UK. Minimum standards must be met and the Government must report to international bodies on the way in which it has fulfilled its obligations for the country as a whole. This will remain the case after the Scottish Parliament has been established. That Parliament will not be able to enact legislation which breaches international human rights standards. If its legislation were to breach the European Convention it could, under the terms of the Human Rights Act, be struck down by the Scottish courts.

Most legislation currently enacted at Westminster applies throughout the UK. On the other hand, the UK has three separate jurisdictions, court and penal systems: in Northern Ireland, in Scotland, and in England and Wales. In some instances, legislation enacted at Westminster for Northern Ireland, and for Scotland, is entirely different from that in England and Wales and the advent of the Scottish Parliament will lead over time to greater differences in the legislation which applies in that part of the country. The jurisdiction of some of the public bodies which concern us here extends across the whole country: the Data Protection Registrar is one example. In Northern Ireland, however, there are usually entirely separate enforcement bodies. In Wales, the Welsh Language Board enforces legislation which does not apply in other parts of the UK. On the other hand, where the jurisdiction of enforcement bodies does cover the whole of Britain they may have regional offices - as the EOC (GB) does in Scotland and in Wales.

Northern Ireland

Northern Ireland has unique problems in protecting human rights because of the persistence of political and religious discrimination and the related civil disorder and political violence which has marred its history since 1921. This is reflected in the powers of the police force and army in Northern Ireland under emergency legislation, in the abolition of jury trial for terrorist offences and in the statutory protection against religious and political discrimination which does not apply in the rest of the UK.

Northern Ireland's unique position is recognised in its distinct legal, court and penal system, and separate public bodies to promote and enforce aspects of human rights. The Fair Employment Commission, which enforces the law against religious and political discrimination, has no counterpart elsewhere in the UK. In addition, Northern Ireland has its own Equal Opportunities Commission, Commission for Racial Equality, Disability Council, Parades Commission, Police Complaints Commission and an Ombudsman whose powers differ from those of his counterparts in Britain. Northern Ireland also has the only quango which makes a contribution to the wider protection of human rights, the Standing Advisory Commission on Human Rights (SACHR). The constraints within which that small advisory body operates were set out in Chapter 2.

The agreement reached between the UK and Irish Governments and the political parties in Northern Ireland on 10 April 1998 included provision for a single Equality Commission comprising the four existing discrimination bodies and a separate Human Rights Commission replacing SACHR. The proposed functions of that body are set out in Chapter 4.

The Standing Advisory Commission on Human Rights argued (prior to Northern Ireland's recent peace agreement) that:

> There is a need for a local body which is both visible and accessible to the Northern Ireland public on the basis that there are a number of specific issues of human rights concern which require specialist knowledge and treatment in the Northern Ireland context. There may, however, be value in the local body also being part of a national human rights framework.[1]

The proposed Human Rights Commission is indeed to be established as a separate Northern Ireland body, initially, at least, with no counterpart in Britain.

Scotland

Scotland also has its own legal, court and penal systems although many of the enforcement bodies, such as the EOC and CRE, cover Scotland as well as England and Wales. Scotland will also soon have its own Parliament with legislative responsibility for a range of policy issues with human rights implications including criminal justice, the police, legal aid, prisons, education and health.

In preparing legislation, the Scottish Executive and Parliament will, like their Westminster counterparts, need advice on the implications of proposed legislation for human rights standards. Members of the public will continue to need advice and assistance if they believe that their rights have been infringed; advice which, in many cases, will require expertise on specifically Scottish law or procedures. A major issue of concern requiring an inquiry may involve legislation specific to Scotland or concern its unique court or penal systems.

The structure of the Human Rights Commission will therefore need to allow for this Scottish dimension. At the 1996 IPPR Consultative Conference, the Chair of the Scottish Council of Civil Liberties also argued that: 'a London – centric UK based Commission would have a battle to establish its credentials'.[2]

Wales

Wales currently shares a legal, court and penal system with England but is run by a separate government department, the Welsh office. A Welsh Assembly is to be established with executive powers in wide areas from local government and education to health. It will inherit the powers of the Secretary of State for Wales to issue guidance and directions in those areas. Wales already hosts separate regional offices of bodies, such as the EOC, which have a British or UK jurisdiction. The existence of the Welsh Language Board reflects the fact that there are human rights issues which are unique to Wales, particularly those relating to the rights of the Welsh minority. It has also been put to us that, while the law, for instance on discrimination, may be the same as in the rest of Britain, it is interpreted and enforced differently. Wales has the highest proportion of jobs in Britain which are segregated by gender and the lowest success rate for sex discrimination cases at industrial tribunals.

When the Welsh Assembly is established, any human rights body seeking to inform and influence its work would need to be seen to be based within Wales. Devolution will lead to greater divergence of policy, and devolution of budgets, to the Assembly. The administrative structures for delivering services are already quite distinct from those in England and are likely to become more so.

Moreover, if a Human Rights Commission is to create a human rights culture, the public will need to feel ownership of its recommendations. A significant proportion of Welsh people are more likely to do so if those recommendations emanate from a Welsh body.

The Children's Rights Office argued that London-based bodies seeking to speak on behalf of the rest of the UK are increasingly criticised because in practice they may only reflect the concerns of England. They can lack the expertise and knowledge from which to represent the interests of those from the other jurisdictions:

> we would be concerned to ensure that Welsh children had the same opportunities as children in the rest of the UK to a Commissioner who was accessible to them, who was directly aware of the issues, concerns and debates affecting them and

who was able to monitor and to promote their rights. A Welsh-based Commissioner linked with Commissioners in the three other jurisdictions would seem to be the most efficient and direct means of ensuring that this could be achieved.[3]

Britain: devolved model

The Commission needs a structure which reflects the new devolved governmental structures while taking into account the need to ensure minimum standards across the whole of the United Kingdom.

We therefore propose that there should be Human Rights Commissions or Commissioners based in England, Wales and Scotland. Together with the Chief Commissioner of the Northern Ireland Commission, the Commissioners in Britain would comprise the UK Commission, chaired by a UK Human Rights Commissioner based in London. The English, Welsh, and Scottish Commissioners would be responsible, within their own parts of the country, for those aspects of the Commission's work which could most effectively be organised at that level.

The UK Commissioner would ensure that the work of the Commissioners was effectively co-ordinated; take responsibility for initiatives which the Commissioners agreed should be organised at the national level; and be primarily responsible for representing the Commission at international fora (although the other Commissioners might equally do so when the issue under discussion was particularly relevant to their work).

Human Rights Commissioners

The Scottish, Welsh and English Human Rights Commissioners should have sufficient staff to provide advice, conduct research, scrutinise legislative proposals, conduct inquiries and promote human rights awareness on those issues specific to their area. In other respects they would draw on the common services provided by the Human Rights Commission in London where it was most efficient or effective to do so. The Commissioners would determine their own priorities, perhaps within the framework set by the Commission as a whole. The Scottish Commissioner would, we anticipate, report to a relevant committee of the new Scottish Parliament as well as, from time to time, to the new

Parliamentary Human Rights Committee at Westminster.

Unlike in Northern Ireland there are, with the exception of the Welsh Language Board, no existing, separate human rights public bodies already located in Scotland or Wales, only regional offices of bodies based in England. Assuming that the CRE and the EOC will, post devolution, continue to cover the whole of Britain, one issue to be resolved would be the relationship between the Human Rights Commissioners and those bodies.

The John Wheatley Centre, a Scottish think-tank, explored the implications of the Scottish Parliament being given responsibility for legislation on equal opportunities. It envisaged that the Parliament would inherit the existing legislation on race, sex and disability, which it could amend within the parameters set by European Community law and wider international human rights standards. The Parliament will not in fact be given responsibility for that legislation but will be able to promote equal opportunities through policy and legislation in the full range of its devolved responsibilities.[4]

Once the Parliament is established, the John Wheatley Centre recommended that separate Scottish equality agencies should be established, 'including' a Scottish EOC, CRE and disability body. It then envisaged the establishment of a Human Rights Commission - presumably a separate Commission for Scotland. It noted that the existing bodies could be brought within the umbrella of the Human Rights Commission but advocated that they remain separate with 'an institutional link and direct relationship'.[5]

Our own view is that any new Scottish equality bodies would be able to promote equality most effectively if they worked within the same structure as the Scottish Human Rights Commissioner. While those bodies continue to have a GB remit, however, the Scottish Parliament could, under the proposed legislation, require them to submit reports or give oral evidence on their work.[6]

Relationship with existing public bodies

The question then arises what the UK Commission's relationship should be with those bodies which are already working in the human rights field such as the EOC and the CRE? As the Lord Chancellor put it when introducing the Human Rights Bill:

> Would a human rights commission take over their responsibilities, or act in partnership with them, or be an independent body independent of them?[7]

In the following analysis, we assume that the current structure of existing bodies is not devolved further but recognise that, were a Welsh or Scottish EOC to be established, for instance, the model we propose would need to be adapted.

In assessing the options, we have taken as our yardstick the need for arrangements which would enhance the effectiveness of the existing bodies as well as ensure the effectiveness of the new Commission. At a time of public expenditure constraints, we have considered the need to obtain value for money, as well as the need to design an organisation which demonstrates transparency and accountability.

In that context we have concluded that there are two options:

- to establish a separate, additional Human Rights Commission; or
- to integrate some existing public bodies within the Commission.

In setting out the arguments for and against these options, we have left to one side the separate issue of the need to reform the legislation which governs the powers of the CREs and the EOCs. In each case we recognise the strength of the case for reform and that it should be a priority for government. It is understandable that it is indeed the first priority for the CREs and the EOCs which have been pressing for reform of their statutes for many years.

The focus of our study, however, was on structure. Our suggestions address the CRE and the EOC with their current powers and jurisdiction. The proposals to amend their legislation, however, were they to be implemented, would not change our analysis or recommendations. They would enhance the ability of those organisations to promote equality but would not shift the balance in our argument on whether those bodies should be left outside of the new Commission or brought within its structure. Were the Government to propose that the equality Commissions (GB) be given new powers to monitor a duty on public sector bodies to promote equality of opportunity, however, as proposed in Northern Ireland, the case for at least creating a single Equality Commission would seem to be unavoidable.

In Chapter 2 we considered the work of a range of existing bodies, not only the equality Commissions and the Data Protection Registrar. In the following analysis, however, we have restricted our consideration to those bodies. They are the principal statutory bodies which promote and enforce human rights standards and would leave the most significant gaps were they to be left outside of the Human Rights Commission.

It has been suggested to us, however, that there are other bodies which ought to be considered as a potential part of that organisation. The Parliamentary and local Ombudsmen, the Broadcasting Standards Authority, the Welsh Language Board (within a Welsh Human Rights Commission), the Prisons' Ombudsman, the Trades Union Commissioner and the new Information Commissioner (under the forthcoming Freedom of Information Act) are some of the suggestions which were made. We have not extended our study to include those options but recognise that, once the principle of a comprehensive Human Rights Commission were accepted, any potential overlap with existing bodies should be examined and the case for widening its membership, or replacing those bodies, considered.

A separate, additional body?

An independent UK Human Rights Commission could be established to work alongside the existing bodies. It would be responsible for promoting and enforcing those human rights issues not covered by their existing mandates. The new Commission would therefore consist only of the Scottish, Welsh and English Commissioners, the Chief Commissioner of the Northern Ireland Commission, and the UK Human Rights Commissioner.

The new Commission might be expected to establish a good working relationship with the existing bodies although there could be tensions if, in its monitoring, promotion or enforcement work it addressed any of the issues for which they are responsible. It might seek to meet regularly with those bodies in the same way that the anti-discrimination bodies in Britain and Ireland meet together now in a forum called the Joint Equality Group. That informal group meets at least twice a year to discuss developments and activities of mutual interest.[8] Within such a network the new Human Rights Commission would be able to exchange information and collaborate on activities.

A separate Commission would be simple and straightforward. It would give the organisation the chance to establish its authority on a range of issues before entering delicate negotiations with existing bodies about changing their structure; and it would leave the existing bodies free to focus on achieving the major changes in their statutes and areas of work which they hope that the Government will bring about. Opting for an independent body would ensure that the Commission could begin work when the Convention is first incorporated, when the law will be most uncertain and its expert advice most needed, while allowing time to consult and plan for its long term relationship with existing bodies.

In the long term, however, there are major disadvantages in leaving discrimination and data protection issues outside of the scope of the Commission. This artificial division of human rights issues into separate organisations does not reflect the reality on the ground. As the Chair of the Scottish Council for Civil Liberties has said:

> human rights exist.., simply the human condition provides you with human rights and these rights are indivisible. You cannot introduce compartments or divisions or prioritise rights. It has to be a holistic approach...[9]

A separate Human Rights Commission would not be able to deal with all aspects of a case when, as is often the case, it concerned more than one human right: for instance, race discrimination (falling within the jurisdiction of the CRE) *and* a denial of the right to family life, or sex discrimination (an EOC matter) which amounted to degrading treatment under the European Convention - a matter for the Human Rights Commission. This situation would be confusing for individuals seeking help and for public bodies and employers seeking guidance or training.

The second disadvantage of this approach is that it would be an inefficient use of public funds. Establishing a separate body would remove the opportunity for efficiency savings which could be released from the sharing of common support services. These might be legal and financial services, training, press and communications, and research and data collection.

As a separate body, the Human Rights Commission could find itself marginalised, overshadowed by the long established equality

Commissions which, despite their narrower briefs, would be likely to have significantly greater resources. Lastly, the Commission would be a small body without any career structure. It might not only be difficult to attract as its Commissioners individuals of the seniority and experience necessary if they are to be authoritative and influential. Its size might also adversely affect its ability to attract and retain high quality staff.

At a private seminar of major British employers organised by Organisation Resource Counselors in November 1997, we were told that human resource departments have policies and procedures on equal opportunities *per se*, not on race equality separately from gender equality and from disability. For their staff it is inconvenient and unhelpful to have to approach three separate organisations to receive information and guidance - 'three separate sets of priorities, Codes of Practice and ten point plans', as one participant put it. In a small survey of some major private sector employers subsequently carried out by ORC (in December 1997), eight out of the ten companies which responded supported the establishment of a Human Rights Commission which would bring the existing equality Commissions within its structure. Levi Strauss and Northern Foods plc made their support public. Comments which were made in support of this proposal included:

> Current arrangement of several commissions is confusing for employers and employees. Bringing it under one body must result in a sharing of expertise and resources and therefore a better service to the customer.

> A one–stop–shop for advice, education and monitoring.

> It would be easier to get co-operation from small firms who currently say that the whole system is just too complex.[10]

Defending the Governments proposal to establish a single Equality Commission in Northern Ireland, Minister Paul Murphy said:

> I take the right hon. Gentleman's point about the one–stop–shop. It makes sense for those who are troubled by matters with which the Equal Opportunities Commission [sic] deals — equal opportunities for women, matters concerning disabled people, fair employment or whatever – to be able to

consult one umbrella organisation to find out how they are affected...[11]

Integration

The alternative to establishing a separate body is thus to integrate the equality Commissions, and potentially other bodies such as the Data Protection Registrar, within the new Commission in some form, to create a body with comprehensive powers and responsibilities. The diagram on page 115 illustrates the options for such a model if some existing, and some new Commissioners, were brought within the Commission.

It would not be feasible to bring together the existing equality Commissions in their current form, in which the principal decision making body is a Commission comprised of up to 15 largely part-time Commissioners. For the equality Commissions to be brought within one structure, the collegiate decision making of each separate Commission would need to be replaced by the collegiate decision making of the full-time Commissioners comprising the Human Rights Commission.

We suggest that the chairs of the CRE and of the EOC, and the Data Protection Registrar, could become named Commissioners of the new body, sharing strategic decision making with the Scottish, Welsh, English and UK Human Rights Commissioners. The Chief Commissioner of the Northern Ireland Human Rights Commission, and indeed of its Equality Commission, would also be potential members of the UK Commission.

The race and sex discrimination statutes in Britain would be amended to convert each collegiate commission into a sole Commissioner whose title would reflect their responsibility - Race Equality Commissioner and Sex (or gender) Equality Commissioner.

The Data Protection Act could, we suggest, also be amended to bring the Privacy (or Data Protection) Commissioner within the Commission. The Data Protection Registrar has expressed the view that:

> Whatever model were to be adopted to give effect to the concept of a Human Rights Commission it would be important that...data protection issues were seen as part of its

> remit. Ensuring data protection is seen as part of a range of
> human rights would be a key advantage. Total integration of
> the existing bodies would be complex, require new legislation
> in all areas and changes in financial structures. As one of the
> smaller players, with grant-in-aid of less than £4 million, I see
> strength in each of the existing bodies retaining its identity
> within the collegiate structure...[12]

Together with the Human Rights Commissioners, those named
Commissioners would form the Human Rights Commission. The Chair
of the new Disability Rights Commission could, similarly, become a
Commissioner of the new body. Over time, the infrastructure of each
body could come together to enable them to share resources and
expertise.

The Race Equality Commissioner, Sex or Gender Equality
Commissioner and Privacy Commissioner would have responsibility
for, and the powers of, their current Commissions unless or until such
time as those powers and responsibilities were accorded by statute to
the Commission as a whole. The Commissioners could, in the short
term, retain their separate location and would, in any event, work to
their own distinct body of legislation. In the long term, separate
locations would limit the extent to which the internal structure of the
Commission could operate efficiently and the extent to which savings
could be made from common services.

Commissioners with specific responsibilities

The proposal that specific, named Commissioners be appointed to take
responsibility for key issues is intended to address the anxiety that the
focus on those issues could be diluted in a generic Commission lacking
such differentiation. In that model, the Commissioners would not have
had specific responsibility and accountability for a particular field of
rights - such as race equality.

We rejected that model although we recognise that it has certain
advantages. It would have provided the greatest opportunity for a
fundamental review and reallocation of the resources of the existing
bodies, enabling the Commissioners to concentrate their resources on
the issues causing greatest concern. It would also enable most advantage
to be made from cost savings achieved by the sharing of common

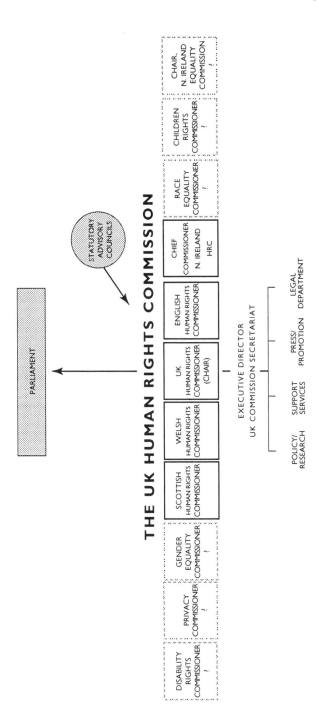

THE UK HUMAN RIGHTS COMMISSION

Options for the structure of a UK Human Rights Commission © IPPR 1998

services. The failure to maintain specific Commissioners for key areas could, however, lead to concern that those issues would be marginalised. Moreover, the communities or groups predominantly concerned with one human rights issue, such as race, would not be able to identify a named Commissioner accountable for that issue with whom to be in dialogue. The energy and focus of the single issue organisations might be lost within a large, undifferentiated body with numerous roles and functions. The EOC argued that amalgamation 'would be recipe for confusion and inefficiency'[13] Openness and transparency could be difficult to achieve, and resources redistributed within the body without public debate about competing priorities. A Commissioner with responsibility for one specific issue would be more likely to maintain the profile of that issue and the resources attached to it. He or she would also provide a clear channel for dialogue with the public and for accountability to Parliament.

The Churches Commission for Racial Justice recognised the advantage of locating responsibility for race equality within a Human Rights Commission - the mutual support that could be offered within a wider Commission and the greater influence it might exert - but only if there were a named Commissioner for racial equality to ensure that the 'cutting edge' of the CRE's work was not lost.[14]

The founding statute should foresee the possible appointment of additional named Commissioners from time to time as the need arose. Early appointments might include a Children's Rights Commissioner. The Children's Rights Office told us that it favours the appointment of such a Commissioner to work either in alliance with a Human Rights Commission or as part of an umbrella organisation, as long as the Commissioner had clear responsibility for his or her own area of work. It was opposed to a structure in which promoting the rights of children was subsumed under a generic workload within a Commission:

> We would not support a proposal in which promoting the rights of children was subsumed under a generic workload within the Human Rights Commission. A central function of any Commissioner for children is to assert the fundamental human rights of children against a tradition of viewing children as either the property of adults or as people in the making. Because the extension of human rights to children is not widely accepted and because children have a low status

and political profile in the UK, their interests are likely to be overlooked if they are directly competing for time and resources with the rights of adults. Children will never be given the recognition and visibility to which they are entitled, without the commitment of an exclusive focus.[15]

The UK is not the first country to have been faced with establishing a Human Rights Commission after there were already a number of single issue organisations in existence. The first Australian Human Rights Commissioner, Brian Burdekin, who was given the task of bringing those organisations within the umbrella of the Human Rights Commission, has argued that there are a number of advantages in having an integrated body rather than separate bodies dealing with different grounds of discrimination and other aspects of human rights. He has written that:

- Connections and similarities between different discrimination issues can be seen more clearly;

- It promotes co-operation between members of disadvantaged groups and gives each an interest in the protection of others;

- Consequently the political position of a Human Rights Commission is made more secure. This can be of considerable importance since it is inevitable that from time to time effective advocacy of human rights will involve disagreement with significant political forces in society;

- Expertise and experience in one area of discrimination, both in legal interpretation and in practical measures, will frequently be relevant in other areas;

- An integrated body makes possible more effective use of resources and specialised expertise, including human rights law.[16]

Perhaps for these reasons, a model which brought the existing bodies within the Human Rights Commission in some form was widely (although not universally) supported by those who responded to our consultation papers. The Immigration Law Practitioners Association, for instance, expressed the view:

> If the purpose is to create a strong presence in national life for the protection of human rights, a single body may be

preferable. Division between different Commissions with separate remits increases the chance of certain types of problems falling through the net. It also lacks the impact of one larger and unified voice. Accordingly a single Commission may be the most effective route to carving out a place for human rights observances in UK political and cultural life.[17]

The advantages which we consider this model would bring are set out below. We then consider the concerns which have been raised about aspects of the model and give the reasons why we consider that those concerns are unfounded.

Advantages of the umbrella body

Bringing the equality Commissions and the Data Protection Registrar within the umbrella of the Human Rights Commission would enable that body to deal with all of the human rights implications of each issue. Whether it was giving legal advice, conducting research or an inquiry, scrutinising draft legislation or promoting awareness, the Commission would be able to include discrimination and data protection issues within the scope of its work.

For those needing information or advice, it would mean a 'one-stop-shop' was available to them. Individuals who believe that they have been the victim of race *and* gender discrimination, or discrimination on grounds of religion *and* disability, or who are unsure on what grounds they were discriminated against, could approach one organisation for help. For employers and for public bodies, equally, it would not be necessary to approach a series of organisations in order to obtain the advice, information or training they need. The Discrimination Law Association argued that the division into separate Commissions is one of the weaknesses of the current system:

> Individuals who may have a combined claim of sex discrimination and/or race discrimination and/or disability discrimination have to go to two or three commissions. This is of particular concern for black women complaining of race and sex discrimination who, at present, must seek help from two separate bodies. (See, for example, *Burton & Rhule v. De Vere Hotels*...in which no claim was made under the Sex

Discrimination Act though it was at least as strong as the claim brought under the Race Relations Act).[18]

Disability Awareness in Action similarly argued:

> Another argument for having one Commission is that several cases of human rights abuse could be seen to be discrimination on several grounds. For many disabled women, for instance, it is hard to know whether they face violation of their rights because they are women or because they are disabled.[19]

The Royal National Institute for Deaf People argued that the authority of each Commission would be strengthened when they spoke together with one voice:

> Experience so far indicates that organisations dealing with discreet aspects of human rights such as discrimination due to gender or race tend to lack public support and political clout and achieve only limited effectiveness in their areas of operation. Since piecemeal change does not appear to have worked very well, there is a strong case, in our view, for comprehensive anti-discrimination legislation to be enforced by an independent Human Rights Commission with a wider brief for tackling all aspects of human rights. Such a body with a large constituency among the public can over time build alliances in the media and in Parliament, and thereby exert significant influence on the Government.[20]

This approach would enable savings to be made from common services so that resources could be reallocated to other areas of work, making more efficient use of public funds. It does not make sense to have five separate press, finance, research and legal departments if those could work more effectively, and cost effectively, together.

This model would help to foster public support for the Commission. The wide range of issues covered, including the rights of elderly people and of children, would help the public to identify with the Commission, in contrast to the hostility or indifference sometimes experienced by the existing single issue bodies. Sir Herman Ouseley, Chair of the CRE, told our consultative conference, for instance, that:

> If one looks at the CRE and its history, part of the problem
> which has bedevilled its credibility is perception. Many if not
> most white people see it as an organisation serving the
> interests only of Black, Asian and other visible minority
> groups.[21]

In its official response to IPPR's proposals, the CRE said that media
hostility was one factor which had led it to consider a possible future
structure in which the equality bodies might form an Equalities
Commission or an 'all encompassing Human Rights Commission'. The
starting point for the CRE would be whether such a structure would
constitute a more effective mechanism to combat racial discrimination
and promote equality of opportunity.[22]

Michael Banton, Chair of the UN's Committee on the Elimination of
Racial Discrimination writing in a personal capacity, said that merger
of the CRE and EOC:

> would help counter the misconception that the Race Relations
> Act privileges the ethnic minorities and would promote
> understanding that racial discrimination is just one form of
> discrimination.[23]

He warned, however, that the merger of the Community Relations
Council and Race Relations Board in the 1970s had been 'pretty
traumatic' so that any merger should be carefully planned.

Significantly, Australia's current Human Rights Commissioner,
Chris Sidoti, told us that the individual Commissioners in Australia's
Commission have been able to make a greater impact than they did
before they were brought together under the umbrella of the Human
Rights and Equal Opportunity Commission in 1986. Racial equality, in
particular, he said, is not seen as special pleading for a minority but as
the enforcement of an internationally protected human right.

Two final advantages of this model both concern its flexibility. First,
it would enable additional Commissioners to be appointed if the
Government wanted to demonstrate that priority was being given to a
particular group, for instance a Commissioner to deal with age
discrimination or with sexual orientation. A number of the responses we
received to our Consultation Paper, including that from the Royal
College of Nursing, argued that a Commissioner with specific

responsibility for children should be appointed within the Commission.

The Royal National Institute for Deaf People argued that a Disability Rights Commission should be established as a separate body initially, until difficulties in enforcing a reformed Disability Discrimination Act had been overcome, but that it should then be 'merged' within the Human Rights Commission:

> ...in the absence of merger, there will be a plethora of Commissions dealing with various aspects of human rights with different remits, functions, powers and procedures. This will be very confusing and frustrating for the potential complainants, especially considering that discrimination due to disability, age, gender and race, frequently overlap. Having a single body responsible for dealing with all aspects of human rights will permit the development of a coherent strategy with a clear focus and priorities among competing objectives, despite its wide brief and diversity of functions.[24]

A generic body would also have the flexibility to take up new issues as they arose and to shift its priorities to reflect current concerns in a way that has not proved possible for single issue organisations with narrow mandates. The inability of the CRE to address the issue of religious discrimination, for instance, because that issue is not covered by the Race Relations Act, illustrates an obstacle which could be overcome by bringing that body within the Human Rights Commission.

During the parliamentary debates on the Human Rights Bill, Baroness Amos, a former chief executive of the EOC argued for an integrated model:

> In my view the effectiveness of the Equal Opportunities Commission and the Commission for Racial Equality would be enhanced by becoming part of a human rights commission. It would bring issues of race and sex discrimination from the margins to the mainstream; the two organisations would no longer be perceived as acting in the interests of a particular social group but would be seen as part of a body promoting and enforcing internationally recognised human rights. For the public, employers and other organisations seeking guidance, there would be a single body: a one-stop-shop.

There will always be difficulties in changing the institutional structure of existing bodies. Reassurance will be needed that the intention is to strengthen each part of any new body and that neither race nor gender discrimination will be marginalised in any new structure. However, differences about optimal structures should not deter us from creating a body which will undoubtedly be needed if the Bill is to achieve its full potential in protecting the rights of people within the United Kingdom.[25]

The Data Protection Registrar, Elizabeth France, agrees that the umbrella model would have significant advantages, although she envisages limits on the extent to which the bodies would be integrated. Writing to Home Office Minister, Lord Williams of Mostyn, she said:

...the concept of an umbrella organisation, with a place on the resulting Commission for the Data Protection Registrar, is one I enthusiastically support. From my perspective the proposals would place data protection clearly on the Human Rights agenda, and would provide better public and Parliamentary scrutiny of the work of my Office, than do current arrangements. The model proposed would not lead to loss of identity of the existing bodies looking after aspects of Human Rights, neither would it be costly to set up or administer. The Australian model, on which it is based, suggests integration should be kept to a minimum with the Commission looking at strategic issues, overlaps and areas of human rights not readily covered by any of the existing bodies.[26]

Six concerns have been raised about the model we have proposed. These are:

- that it does not integrate the work of the separate bodies sufficiently;

- that the issues covered by the existing bodies could be diluted and marginalised within a broader Commission;

- that the existing bodies might lose out in the competition for resources in a Commission addressing a wider range of issues;

- that those currently represented on the multi-member equality Commissions would lose their position of influence;

- that time-consuming negotiations now about new structures would divert the equality Commissions from working to secure the policy and legislative changes which they hope that the new Government will deliver; and

- that being brought within the Human Rights Commission would, over time, mean that the EOC and the Data Protection Registrar's Office would have to relocate.

We consider each of these concerns in turn:

Insufficient integration?

The Law Society was concerned that the umbrella structure, while providing for some flexibility, still retains distinctions between discreet areas of discrimination. It suggested that we consider as an alternative:

a model for the structure for the new Commission based not on legal definitions of areas of discrimination, each with their own separate administration but based on the way discrimination impacts - and indeed the way that many anti-discrimination statutes are drawn: a simple structure based on advice and assistance for employment issues, and advice and assistance for goods and services issues. This might be more efficient than the 'vertical' structure, for legal departments at least and could relate better to the way discrimination is experienced by individuals and to the areas where advice and help are needed and sought by employers and business...[27]

The Discrimination Law Association, however, argued:

that within the single organisation responsibility for particular areas of discrimination, such as are represented by the current commissions, must be delegated to a distinct section or department. The reason is that the practical context of each type of discrimination and the kind of problem which arise within it may be very different and require special skills and experience.[28]

The Law Society suggested that the umbrella model might nevertheless be useful as a step towards achieving the level of integration it wanted to see. The answer here may be that these issues are ones of internal structure, below the level of Commissioners, and not dependent on whether there are named Commissioners for specific areas of discrimination on the lines we have proposed.

Marginal issues?

Some of the existing equality Commissions and those who work closely with them have expressed concern that some issues could be marginalised within the new body. Each believe that their issue is unpopular and would be overshadowed by others. This concern has equally been voiced in relation to the proposed Northern Ireland Equality Commission.

Our proposal that the existing Commissions continue to be represented by a specific Commissioner who could argue for priority for that issue is intended to overcome this concern, although we consider that there is little danger that race or gender would be marginalised. On the contrary, race and gender discrimination would come into the UK Commission with substantial budgets, around £15 million (1997-8) and £6 million respectively. Each has an articulate community to speak out were there any suggestion that their issue were being down-graded. Each of those issues also has its own specific legislation imposing statutory requirements on employers, service providers and the Commissioners themselves. A Disability Rights Commissioner would find him or herself in a similar position, assuming that a separate Commission had, as proposed, already been established. Of greater concern should be whether those issues falling within the brief of the Human Rights Commissioners, such as censorship, religious freedom or age discrimination would always get the priority they merit.

The Chairman of the CRE suggested that concern about dilution might be alleviated if a separate Human Rights Commission were established first, taking in the existing bodies at a later stage:

> Undoubtedly...there is a strong case for a single anti-discrimination body bringing the issues of age, disability, sexuality, appearance and religion into line with race and gender. But there would be significant issues, concerns and anxieties to be overcome. Some of the different communities and interest groups affected would be concerned about being marginalised... It may therefore be preferable, initially, to have a Human Rights Commission that focuses on ECHR issues,

with a commitment to absorb the other discrimination issues on a phased basis, provided that it can be seen as successful within a specific period of time.[29]

The Chairwoman of the EOC, Kamlesh Bahl, considered that an umbrella body might, however:

> lead to confused priorities with a loss of focus. Issues on sex equality, such as helping women reconcile work and family, are not the same as those concerned with racism or disability discrimination which require different strategies.[30]

The EOC believes that its single issue focus has been vital to its success.[31]

This concern does not seem to be well founded. Many organisations, in the public and the private sector, cover a range of issues for which they need to adopt different strategies. Even within the existing single issue Commissions, entirely different strategies are needed, for instance promoting good practice within companies on the one hand while operating a test-case strategy to clarify the law. The Commissioners on the Human Rights Commission would be well equipped to identify the different strategies needed on different issues; but they would also be able, by working together, to adopt strategies which address more than one issue, for instance, to tackle all aspects of discrimination in circumstances where that is appropriate.

Disability Awareness in Action argued for an umbrella model, precisely so that disability issues would not be marginalised:

> We believe that the collegiate approach with commissioners representing different issues - gender, race, disability etc. - should be implemented. This is particularly imperative for disability. Experience has shown that whatever the legal base and whatever good intentions, disabled people's rights are marginalised by other groups or within issues... It is also often the case that when there are separate commissions that the disability section gets less financial support or less political teeth... We recognise that the present Commissions in the UK may find a new structure difficult to handle initially, but in the interests of human rights for all we believe that this is the most efficient and collaborative mechanism.[32]

The Royal National Institute for Deaf People argued similarly that a single body responsible for dealing with all aspects of human rights need not lead to a loss of focus on any single issue:

> ...focus, as well as the energy and drive of an organisation depend, in the ultimate analysis, upon the quality of its leadership.[33]

Competition for resources?

The Northern Ireland EOC expressed concern that the new ECHR rights might lose out in competition with those coming within the remit of the existing bodies. Who, it asked, would determine the 'severity' of the issue and hence resource allocation?[33] Others were concerned that the budgets of the existing bodies would effectively be cut.

That there would be competition for resources within the Commission is undoubtedly true, and rightly so. The Commissioners would have to decide what the priorities of the organisation should be and allocate their resources accordingly. This would be in contrast to the current system of resource allocation in which the budgets of the existing bodies are determined by separate government departments with little public debate about the choices made. While some fear that their issue might lose out, others would welcome the acknowledgement of the need to prioritise issues. Whether current issues did indeed lose out would depend, as now, on whether the Convention issues covered by the generic Human Rights Commissioners - fair hearing, religious freedom, censorship and so forth - attracted adequate additional funding. The Data Protection Registrar rightly warns however that the difficulty with amalgamating budgets is ensuring that there are no players so dominant that others suffer atrophy.[35] That is not only a matter of personalities but of structure and procedures. The experience of the Australian Commission, in which there have sometimes been tensions over resource allocation, suggests that the collegiate decision making structure should be one designed to foster consensus, not division.

Loss of multi-member lay Commissions

In our view, this is an issue which revolves around openness and accountability, as well as expertise. Each of the existing equality

Commissions is run by a multi-member Commission, allowing direct involvement by some concerned organisations and individuals in the decisions of the Commission. In the umbrella model, those Commissioners would be replaced by a single Commissioner who would make strategic and resource decisions with their fellow executive Commissioners on the Human Rights Commission. The current members of the equality Commissions would therefore no longer be members of those decision-making bodies but of the statutory advisory councils which we advocate (below) which would draw on a wider range of interested parties and expertise.

There are costs and benefits of this approach. The multi-member Commission model has brought some expert lay Commissioners into positions where they make a significant contribution to the organisation. It has given influence and responsibility to a limited number of individuals. On the other hand, these unelected Commissions are closed and unaccountable to the public at large.

The advisory council model set out below, drawing on a far wider range of interests for open debates, in which the Commissioners would explain their decisions and priorities, could considerably enhance transparency and public debate. They would provide a means of accountability to the public which would complement the new mechanisms we propose of parliamentary accountability to elected representatives.

Time-consuming negotiations?

This concern had greater validity when the question was whether a Human Rights Commission should be established by the Human Rights Act. In the immediate aftermath of the election, the equality Commissions were naturally concerned to give priority to ensuring that the Government was aware of their agenda and to commit their resources to securing legislative and policy reform.

Reform of the equality legislation and the establishment of an integrated Human Rights Commission could now be planned in parallel. It would be logical to consider reform of the structure of the equality Commissions at the same time as considering reform of the legislation under which they operate. It would indeed provide the opportunity to consider reform of each piece of equality legislation to harmonise their provisions where appropriate, and to consider whether it would be desirable to vest responsibility for the enforcement of the legislation in the Human Rights Commission as a whole rather than separately with each Commissioner.

There is therefore a case for linking consideration of the umbrella structure to a comprehensive review of the present laws protecting and promoting equality. Without such a review and the legal reforms it would be likely to recommend, organisational change may tackle only part of the problem and its potential be only partly realised. No amount of new structures or forms of organisation will resolve the difficulties currently experienced by the CRE and the EOC that stem from the weakness of their current powers or limits to the scope of the law they enforce. Thus, the Commission for Racial Equality warns:

> To bring the existing discrimination bodies under one roof - or one umbrella - without enactment of new equality legislation would not achieve..... integration. The inadequacies of the Race Relations Act would remain; the new structure on its own would not fill the gaps or strengthen enforcement powers.[36]

Relocation costs?

In the long run, it would be desirable to bring the separate bodies together at one location. Only in that way could the departments be integrated and work effectively together. However, the Government would need to consider the extent to which the Commission would need regional offices in order to be accessible to the public. The future role of the local Racial Equality Councils could also be considered in that context. Given that there would be a strong case for regional offices and indeed the EOC and CRE already has them, some of the staff currently in the North West might expect to be able to remain there while others might be able to relocate to offices outside of London.

Independence and Accountability

The UN guidance on national institutions states that the body should:

> ...be granted a separate and distinct legal personality of a nature which will permit it to exercise independent decision-

making power. Independent legal status should be of a level sufficient to permit an institution to perform its functions without interference or obstruction from any branch of government or any public or private entity.[37]

In this section we therefore first consider the Commission's relationship with Government and with Parliament - how to find the appropriate balance between independence and accountability. We then look, however, at a mechanism for ensuring that there is also accountability to the public whose rights the Commission would exist to protect.

A Government Consultation Paper *Opening Up Quangos* in 1997 pointed to the need to make quangos more open, accountable and effective. Our proposals are in line with those objectives and mirror some of its suggestions. [38]

Relationship with government

The key requirement of human rights institutions in the UN's Paris Principles is that of independence from government. The Commission should be free from government control and independent of party politics; must be able to act on its own initiative and be subject to financial arrangements which give it the greatest possible freedom to determine its own priorities, subject to safeguards to ensure financial probity.

The Commission is perhaps most likely to be established by legislation originating in the Home Office. Two of the bodies which may be brought at some stage within the Commission, the CRE and the Data Protection Registrar, also fall under that department. The EOC, however, falls under the Department for Education and Employment, as does the proposed Disability Rights Commission. Children's right, are the responsibility of the Department of Health.

Once it has been established, it would be possible for the Human Rights Commission not to be accountable to the Home Office nor to any government department, except in relation to its financial arrangements. Its resources could be provided directly from the Consolidated Fund, as are those of Parliamentary Ombudsman. That relationship would not prevent Ministers from asking the Commission to investigate an issue of public concern.

In practice, the quality of the Commission's day to day relationship with government and Whitehall would be a key determinant of its influence. The Children's Rights Office argues:

> Human Rights Commissioners are most likely to attain
> influence through the establishment of positive formal and
> informal relationships with Ministers and civil servants as well
> as key figures in other public bodies.[39]

The New Zealand Human Rights Commission and New Zealand's
Minister of Justice recently agreed a Memorandum of Agreement setting
out the terms of their working relationship (See chapter 3). A 'non-
statutory memorandum of understanding' is similarly to be agreed
between the Government and the Northern Ireland Human Rights
Commission on 'various administrative matters'.

Relationship with Parliament

We perceive that the body's primary responsibility will be owed to
Parliament and, in particular, to the proposed Parliamentary Committee
on Human Rights. Such a Committee was suggested in the Labour
Party's pre-election Consultation Paper *Bringing Rights Home*.[40] The
roles for the Committee were expected to be these:

- to monitor the operation of the new Act and other aspects of the
  UK's human rights obligations;

- to scrutinise new legislation where this was identified as having
  an impact on human rights issues.

It was proposed that the Committee be made up of members of both
Houses and that it have the powers of a Select Committee to call for
papers and to compel the attendance of witnesses to give evidence. The
White Paper accompanying the Human Rights Bill gave further impetus
to this proposal, suggesting that the Committee could be a Joint
Committee of both Houses of Parliament or that each House might
have its own Committee. The Committee might conduct inquiries on
issues relating to the Convention, produce reports to assist the
Government and Parliament in deciding what action to take, and
examine issues relating to the UK's other international obligations.

When this Committee is established the Commission should have a
close working relationship with it, providing it with expert opinion and
reporting on its own work and concerns. The relationship could develop

along the lines of that which the Parliamentary Commissioner for Administration has with the Commons Public Administration Committee. We envisage the Committee, on occasion, asking the Human Rights Commission to investigate particular matters which were causing concern or which it did not itself have the resources or expertise to examine. The Consultation Paper *Opening Up Quangos* suggested that Select Committees might play a more systematic role in reviewing the work of those bodies.

The Commission should present an annual report to the Committee and report to it from time to time on particular issues. Moreover, each of the Commissioners should report on the issues within their responsibility. It is to be hoped that this Committee could give greater attention to the work of the Commission than existing Select Committees have always been able to do to the work of the CRE, EOC and the Data Protection Registrar.

Appointment of Commissioners

The UN guidance advises that Commissioners should be appointed by a procedure which ensures their independence, recommending that appointments be made by Parliament. The priority should also be an appointment system which ensures that Commissioners are appointed because they have the expertise and skills required for the post, not because they are perceived by Government, or a political party, as sympathetic to their political objectives. The Nolan Committee recommended that appointments should be made on the basis of merit but should also take into account the need for a balance of relevant skills, interests and 'backgrounds'. Although Nolan did not refer to the need to include ethnicity or disability within the term 'background', such consideration would seem to be compatible with his recommendations and would certainly be essential in relation to the Human Rights Commission, as to other quangos. The Good Friday Agreement states that the Commissioners on the Northern Ireland Human Rights Commission will reflect the community balance in Northern Ireland. That balance should extend beyond the religious communities to gender, race and disability.

In the absence of a Public Appointments Commission which would shield such appointments from direct political control, we recommend that Commissioners should be appointed by the Crown with the approval of Parliament. That approval, in practice, could perhaps be exercised by endorsement or veto by the Parliamentary Human Rights Committee.

The Nolan Committee considered and rejected the idea that such public appointments could be made not by a Minister but by an independent body. It argued that 'in order to retain accountability to Parliament, a Minister must retain responsibility for making appointments and, where problems arise for terminating them'.[41] It did not appear to consider the dual system of appointments by the Crown, endorsed by Parliament, used in a number of countries for the appointment of Human Rights Commissioners. This approach would provide some safeguard against political criteria dominating the appointment process.

Appointment of Commissioners should be for a fixed, renewable term. Their dismissal, on grounds set out in the statute, should be only with the approval of both Houses of Parliament, as is the case now for the Data Protection Registrar. The Northern Ireland Bill gives the power of appointment and dismissal of Commissioners to the Secretary of State.

Relationship with advisory councils

There are many organisations and individuals who will have a direct interest in the work of the Commission. Voluntary organisations, trade unions and employers, professional bodies, community groups, academics, local authorities and agencies such as the police and prison service will want to be consulted about the priorities of the Commission and of individual Commissioners and on the approach they intend to adopt on different issues. The Commission, in turn, will need dialogue with those organisations and individuals to help it stay closely in touch with changing issues on the ground, to contribute their views on the appropriate balance to be found between competing priorities, and as partners in joint initiatives.

The UN principles stress the importance of involving individuals from all sections of society in the Commission. One way to do this would be to create a statutory advisory council for the Commission, with a broad membership, which would meet regularly with the Human Rights Commissioners and his or her colleagues. Advisory councils alternatively could be established for each region or key policy area.

The Commission should decide whom to invite and accept as members of the advisory councils but, in so doing, should be required to bear in mind the need for the councils to reflect the diversity of communities and the range of views on human rights issues. It should, in our view, also ensure representation of those public bodies whose decisions or practices may on occasion be the subject of concern so that the HRC is, and is seen to be, in a position to take an informed view. It should also draw representatives from across the country and the meetings could be held in different parts of the country to facilitate their attendance.

Transparency is one important element of accountability. It should be possible for non-members of the council to attend as observers; minutes of the meetings should be accessible to the public and key issues arising from the meetings could be referred to in the HRC's annual report. The Consultation Paper *Opening Up Quangos* suggested that quangos should hold public meetings and release a summary report on what took place.

The role of NGOs

Non-governmental organisations which provide advice on human rights issues, take test cases, conduct research or campaign will want to know that the Commission will complement their work, not seek to replace it. A constructive and co-operative relationship will be essential. Commissions overseas have conducted research jointly with NGOs, drawn on their expertise in responding to draft international Conventions, and relied on NGO's assistance in encouraging individuals to give evidence to their inquiries (see Chapter 3).

The UN guidelines on establishing Human Rights Commissions stress the importance of working with NGOs. The Paris Principles provide that:

> In view of the fundamental role played by non-governmental organisations in expanding the work of national institutions, national institutions shall develop relations with non-governmental organisations devoted to promoting and protecting human rights, to economic and social development, to combating racism, to protecting particularly vulnerable groups (especially children, migrant workers, refugees, physically and mentally disabled persons) or to specialised areas.'[42]

Internal structure of the Commission

The internal structure of the Commission would depend on the decision whether to bring the existing Commissions within its umbrella, whether to create one or more new Commissioners (for example, on children's rights) and on the timing of those decisions - whether those bodies are brought in at the beginning or after the HRC has been established.

The diagram (page 115) illustrates the possible final structure of the Commission after some existing and new Commissioners had been brought within its umbrella.

We described above the collegiate decision making structure of the Commission. We envisage that the organisation would be run by a chief executive, accountable to the UK Human Rights Commissioner, although on a day-to-day basis he or she could deal directly with individual Commissioners on particular issues. The heads of the departments of the Commission would in turn be accountable to the chief executive. For the purpose of illustrating the model we envisage that there might be four departments:

- *Legal department*: providing legal advice and assistance to individuals, responsible for litigation and for scrutiny of proposed and existing legislation for conformity to international human rights standards. The department could be internally differentiated into specialist sections, such as different kinds of discrimination (as in the case in the Australian Commission).

- *Research and policy department*: responsible for developing the policy of the Commission, for conducting inquiries and for commissioning and conducting research.

- *Press and promotion*: responsible for publications, promotion material and relations with the press and media.

- *Support services*: finance, personnel, staff training and central administration.

Where there are specialist services within one of the existing bodies, such as the registration functions of the Data Protection Registrar, it may be appropriate for those functions to remain directly accountable to the Commissioner to whom they relate.

Implementation

A Human Rights Commission must be a statutory body, established by primary legislation that sets out its powers and responsibilities. Any changes to the structure of the existing Commissions or to that of the Data Protection Registrar would also require primary legislation.

The Commission could be established in stages, beginning with the appointment of a Human Rights Commissioner who could have a duty to consult and then advise Government on the future relationship between his or her office and the existing statutory bodies in the human rights field.

An alternative interim proposal is that the Commissioner should be joined by the heads of the existing bodies sitting as Commissioners in an ex-officio capacity. They would make decisions on a collegiate basis about the work of the Commission without affecting the autonomy of their own organisation. The Disability Rights Commission and a Children's Rights Commissioner, if appointed, could equally be part of that loose relationship.

Neither of these arrangements would fulfil the objectives we have set out in the long term but could form interim steps in an evolving process of structural change.

Finance

Assuming that, in its first year, the Commission would be a separate, additional body, we asked a former Under Secretary at the Home Office to estimate the potential cost of the body for that year. The estimate he prepared, and the assumptions on which it is based are in Appendix 3. Calculating that the Commission would initially need 40 staff, he estimated that the full cost of the Commission in its first full year would be £2.8M. In subsequent years he anticipated that expenditure would be greater, as did some of those who responded to our Consultation paper. The budget of the Northern Ireland Human Rights Commission in its first year has been set at only £750,000.

We invited comments on whether the Commission could seek to raise some of its funds from charitable foundations or the private sector, noting that the CRE, for instance, has done so. The CRE estimates that financial support 'in kind', such as free advertising space, amounts to around £750,000 p.a. In addition it received, in 1997, somewhat less than £100,000 in cash donations, for instance in sponsorship of its 'Race in the Media' awards. While some of those who responded feared that such external funding could compromise the Human Rights Commission's independence, others endorsed the suggestion with the proviso that care should be taken to ensure that no strings were attached.

The Immigration Law Practitioners' Association:

> financing should be primarily, if not exclusively from the public purse and guaranteed in such a way as to limit so far as possible any political interference as regards allocation of resources.[43]

Barrister Rabinder Singh argued that it should accept private funding - but only from charitable foundations:

> If, say, newspaper proprietors could make large donations to the Commission, its perceived independence might be undermined and the fear that human rights such as freedom of speech tend in practice to be the preserve of the rich and powerful would be given some credibility.[44]

Home Office Minister, Lord Williams of Mostyn, was pressed during the Parliamentary debates to say whether the Treasury would veto a proposal for a new Commission - in essence whether public expenditure constraints were a major obstacle. His reply suggested that the sums involved would be no obstacle were the political will there to establish the Commission:

> I do not readily understand that anyone would be able successfully to overrule the Lord Chancellor and the Home Secretary if they concluded that they wanted public funding, but that is a little way down the road. The question was whether there will be a Treasury veto. I shall try again: no, no, no.[45]

The Data Protection Registrar has been frustrated by a restriction on her charging for any advice or service provided by her office to organisations:

> Advice is vital...If adequate resources are to be available for

this role then the ability to recover costs in some way though an element of the education and promotion functions seems to me essential.[46]

Conclusion

In this chapter we have considered three separate structural questions: the extent to which, in line with devolution, the Commission should have a structure which is devolved in Scotland, Wales and England; the relationship which the Commission might have with existing statutory bodies working in the human rights field; and finally its relationship with government, with Parliament and with non-governmental organisations and the public.

We noted, first, that the Northern Ireland Bill includes provision for the establishment of a Human Rights Commission in Northern Ireland. The UK Government is accountable under international law for ensuring that minimum human rights standards are met throughout the United Kingdom and needs to ensure a degree of uniformity in the protection of human rights in all parts of the UK. It may therefore be desirable for the Northern Ireland Commission to have a formal relationship with its counterparts in Britain. We proposed that its Chief Commissioner should be a member of the UK Commission.

We concluded that, for a number of reasons it would not be appropriate to have a single Human Rights Commission covering the whole of Britain. Separate Human Rights Commissioners should be appointed for Scotland, Wales and England, chaired by a UK Human Rights Commissioner based in London. The UK Human Rights Commissioner would take responsibility for those functions of the Commission which could not be devolved to the regional level.

In relation to existing statutory bodies working in the human rights field, we concluded that it would be feasible to establish the Human Rights Commission as a separate, additional body (as is currently proposed in Northern Ireland). The Human Rights Commissioners would work alongside their counterparts in the equality Commissions and bodies such as the Data Protection Registrar, liaising with them where their interests overlapped. The heads of those bodies could be appointed ex-officio Commissioners of the Human Rights Commission to facilitate such co-operation. However we concluded that, for many reasons, this would not, in the long term, prove to be the most effective, nor most cost effective model.

We argued that there could be significant advantages in the Human Rights Commission bringing within its umbrella, in some form, the existing equality Commissions and the proposed Disability Rights Commission. We also suggested that the Data Protection Registrar could usefully come within the remit of the Commission, as the current Registrar has herself argued, and that the possible inclusion of a number of other organisations should be considered were the principle of an overarching Human Rights Commission to be accepted.

In Northern Ireland the Government should, for the same reasons, consider carefully whether the Human Rights Commission should be established separately from the proposed Equality Commission. There would be many occasions on which an issue investigated by the Human Rights Commission would involve issues of discrimination and the organisations might most effectively operate as a single body.

We did not propose that the existing statutory bodies in Britain should be *merged* within the broader Human Rights Commission. Rather, we suggested that the heads of each body could be appointed as named Commissioners, retaining their current statutory responsibilities unless or until those responsibilities were invested in the new body of Commissioners as a whole. The full Human Rights Commission could thus comprise; the UK, Scottish, Welsh and English Human Rights Commissioners; the Chief Commissioner of the Northern Ireland Human Rights Commission; the Race Equality Commissioner, Gender Equality Commissioner, Privacy Commissioner, Disability Rights Commissioner and Children's Rights Commissioner.

We set out the series of advantages which we foresaw in bringing existing bodies within the umbrella of the Human Rights Commission: that it would provide a 'one-stop-shop' for individuals, employers and public bodies and enable the Commission to deal with all aspects of a case; that it would enhance the status, public acceptability and influence of the existing single-issue bodies; that it would enable savings to be made from common services; that it would enable additional Commissioners to be appointed if the Government wanted to demonstrate that priority was being given to a particular issue or group (such as older people or children); and that, unlike single issue organisations, it would have the flexibility to shift its resources and priorities onto new issues of concern as they arose.

We also addressed the concerns that have been expressed about that approach; that it would provide insufficient integration; that it would lead to competition for resources; that it would entail the loss of the multi-member lay commissions; that it would involve time-consuming negotiations among the existing bodies and entail relocation costs; answering each of those concerns in turn.

The Commission must be a statutory body established by primary legislation setting out its powers and responsibilities. It could, however, be established in stages, beginning with the appointment of one or more of the Human Rights Commissioners, entirely separate from the structure of existing bodies. The Commissioner(s) could be given the responsibility to consult, and advise the government and Parliament, on the long term options for the structure of the Commission, leading to further legislation at a later stage.

Finally, we looked at the questions of independence and of accountability. We noted that the UN's *Paris Principles* set down ground rules for the relationship between the Commission and the government, requiring that the Commission should have sufficient independence to enable it to fulfil its functions without direction or interference. We suggested that the Commissioners should be appointed by the Crown but with the approval of Parliament - in practice that of the Parliamentary Human Rights Committee - and should be dismissable only by both Houses of Parliament on specific grounds, as is the case for the Data Protection Registrar now. The government could ask the Commission to look in to particular issues but the Commission should not be subject to any direction by government in the way in which it fulfils its functions, other than for its financial probity. Within the overall budget agreed by Parliament, it should be able to determine the allocation of its resources.

We envisaged a close relationship between the Commission and Parliament. Like its counterparts, particularly in the Old Commonwealth, the Commission could regularly be called upon to advise Select Committees, in particular the proposed Human Rights Committee, and report regularly to that Committee on its work and priorities. The Committee might ask the Commission to investigate and report to it on particular issues.

It would also be important for the work of the Commission to be transparent to the public and for there to be a regular dialogue between the Commissioners and those statutory bodies and non-governmental bodies most concerned with its work. We therefore recommended that statutory advisory bodies might be appointed with a broad membership. They should meet regularly with the Commissioners, holding their meetings in different parts of the country.

Were the Commission to be established as a separate body its cost in its first year, with 40 staff, would be in the region of £2.8 million. The Commission could legitimately, in our view, raise additional funds from private and charitable sources for specific research, education or promotion activities. It could also charge some organisations for its training and advisory service.

Endnotes

1. Response of SACHR to the IPPR Consultation Paper, 11 February 1997.

2. Alan Miller, Scottish Council for Civil Liberties, IPPR Conference, London 18 December 1996.

3. Response from the Children's Rights Office to IPPR Consultation Paper, 25 February 1997.

4. Scotland's Parliament, cm 3658, White Paper, July 1997, para 2-5.

5. *Equal opportunities Under a Scottish Parliament* John Wheatley Centre (1997).

6. White Paper, cm 3658, *op cit.,* para 2-10.

7. Second Reading Human Rights Bill, HL 3 November 1997, col.1233.

8. Joint liaison and joint actions also take place at a more informal level. EOC (NI) Submission to IPPR, August 1997.

9. Alan Miller, Chair, Scottish Council for Civil Liberties, IPPR Conference, London, 18 December 1996.

10. Letter to Sarah Spencer from Elizabeth Melling of Organisation Resources Counselors Inc. setting out the results of the survey, dated 15 January 1998.

11. Second Reading Northern Ireland Bill, HC 20 July 1998, col 877.

12. Data Protection Registrar, Options Paper on a Human Rights Commission for the UK, London, 18 December 1996. Largely reproduced as Appendix 12 to the 13th Annual Report of the Data

protection Registrar, 1997.

13. Response to IPPR proposals, 29 July 1997.

14. Letter to authors from Revd.David Haslam, 11 February 1997.

15. Response to IPPR consultation paper, 25.2.97.

16. Burdekin, B, *Human Rights Commissions*, a paper prepared for the Meeting of National Human Rights Institutions convened in Paris, 7-9 October 1991.

17. Immigration Law Practitioner's Association, response to IPPR Consultation Paper, 28 February 1997.

18. Comments on the IPPR Consultation Paper, 17.4.97.

19. Disability Awareness in Action Response to IPPR Consultation Paper, 8 January 1997.

20. RNID response to IPPR Consultation paper, 12 February 1997

21. Herman Ouseley speaking on 18 December 1996.

22. *Incorporation of the ECHR into UK law: Implications for Racial Equality and the work of the CRE.* July 1997.

23. Letter to authors, 19 December 1996.

24. RNID, response to IPPR Consultation Paper, 12 February 1997

25. HL Second Reading, 3 November 1997, col 1248.

26. Letter to Lord Williams of Mostyn, Home Office Minister, 15 May 1997.

27. Response by the Law Society Employment Law Committee, September 1997.

28. Comments from the Discrimination Law Association on the IPPR Consultation Paper.

29. Herman Ouseley speaking to IPPR consultative conference, 18 December 1996.

30. Equal Opportunities Commission, Submission to IPPR, 29 July 1997.

31. Bahl, K, 'An Umbrella body would lead to a loss of focus'. *Guardian* 12 August 1997.

32. Disability Awareness in Action response to IPPR Consultation Paper, 8 January 1997.

33. RNID Response to IPPR Consultation Paper, February 1997.

34. EOC (NI) *Comments on IPPR Proposal for a Human Rights Commission.* July 1997.

35. Letter to the authors, 19 December 1997.

36. Commission for Racial Equality, submission to IPPR, August 1997.

37. National Human Rights Institutions, A Handbook, (1995) para 70.

38. Cabinet Office, November 1997.

39. Response to IPPR Consultation Paper, 25 February 1997.

40. *'Bringing Rights Home' op.cit.*

41. *Standards in Public Life,* cm 2850-1, 1995, Volume 1: Report.

42. See Appendix 1.

43. Response to IPPR Consultation Paper, 28 February 1997.

44. Response to IPPR Consultation Paper, 13 February 1997.

45. Second Reading of the Human Rights Bill, HL 3 November 1997, col 1309.

46. 'A Human Rights Commission for the UK – The options'. Appendix 12 to the 13th Annual Report of the Data Protection Registrar, 1997.

6. Conclusion

A Human Rights Commission is to be established in Northern Ireland. The Government has indicated that it has an open mind on whether such a Commission might be established in Britain after the Human Rights Act has come into force. It has stated that it would want to see greater consideration given, and greater consensus on, the functions which a Human Rights Commission would fulfil and particularly on the relationship which it would have with existing statutory bodies working in the human rights field. This report has considered, and made recommendations on, the functions of the Commission and the options for its structure.

In the Introduction, we reviewed the political context of the proposal in Britain, Northern Ireland and internationally. We noted the support for a Human Rights Commission in Parliament; noted certain parallel developments taking place - the proposed establishment of a Parliamentary Human Rights Committee; the anticipated Disability Rights Commission and the appointment of an Information Commissioner under the Freedom of Information Act. We also pointed to the compromise proposal raised in Parliament: that a Human Rights Commissioner be appointed prior to the Human Rights Act coming into force, to work separately from the existing statutory bodies. That Commissioner could have a duty to consult, and to advise the Government and Parliament, on the options for the long term relationship between his or her office and the existing statutory bodies, in particular with the equality Commissions.

In Chapter Two we assessed the uneven state of human rights protection in the UK. Most of the international human rights standards binding on the UK have not been incorporated into domestic law and can only be enforced, if at all, through a weak international supervisory procedure. We reviewed the protection provided by domestic law, taking into account the significant new safeguards provided by the Human Rights Act, and found that protection remains patchy, not least for certain vulnerable groups such as children and the elderly. We drew attention not only to the uneven protection provided by law but also to the importance of *access* to justice; of measures taken to *prevent* human rights abuses - including the need for effective scrutiny of draft legislation and policy in Whitehall and Parliament - and of the need to raise public awareness of human rights standards so that people adopt those standards not only within the institutions in which they work but also in their daily lives.

Finally, we looked at the public bodies which contribute to the prevention and enforcement of human rights standards, in particular at the Standing Advisory Commission on Human Rights in Northern Ireland and at the equality Commissions. We acknowledged the significant contribution which those Commissions make but noted that their limited mandates would prevent them fulfilling the new challenges presented by the Human Rights Act: advice, scrutiny, investigation and promotion functions in relation to the wide range of human rights in the European Convention on Human Rights which fall almost entirely outside of their statutory remit. We considered whether those new functions could be carried out by the proposed Parliamentary Human Rights Committee and concluded that, while that Committee had a key role to play, it could not undertake the wide range of roles which could be performed by an independent statutory body.

In Chapter Three we noted that the United Nations is pressing member states to establish national institutions for the protection and promotion of human rights, as is the Council of Europe. The UN has set down guidelines to guarantee the independence and effectiveness of such bodies, known as the *Paris Principles,* but these provide only a broad framework within which it is a matter for each member state to determine the form which its national human rights institution should take. There is a growing number of such bodies throughout the world and, recognising the contribution which they can make, the UK government has given technical assistance to a number of those most recently established.

We reviewed the functions and structure of some of the more established Commissions, particularly those in the Commonwealth, and gave examples of their work and achievements. There are not necessarily any direct lessons for the UK from their varied experience but there are many practical ideas from which we could benefit.

In Chapter 4 we considered the range of roles which the Northern Ireland Human Rights Commission and a UK Commission might be expected to fulfil, drawing on many of the responses which we had received to a consultation paper. We argued that the Commission should have a broad mandate, drawing on international human rights standards, not only on the limited European Convention on Human Rights. In relation to specific functions, we noted that opinions differ on where the emphasis should lie: whether the primary focus should be on ensuring access to justice, on taking test cases to clarify the law and on investigating human rights abuses; or whether priority should be given to promoting good practice and awareness of human rights principles. Nevertheless, while the emphasis differed, we found broad support for the view that the Commission should have all of those functions.

Under the heading of prevention, we set out the key functions which the Commission should fulfil. It should promote good practice within those public bodies (and private bodies fulfilling public functions) covered by the Human Rights Act; making them aware of their new obligations so that they might adapt their policies and behaviour in order to comply and avoid the need for litigation.

Secondly, the Commission should promote awareness of human rights principles among the public, through the media and by working with the curricula authorities to ensure that these principles are central to education for citizenship in schools.

Thirdly, the Commission should scrutinise draft legislation and policy and advise the government, and Parliament, of any provisions which might breach international human rights standards, in particular those of the European Convention. This role will be no less necessary when Ministers, under the provisions of the Human Rights Act, are required to inform Parliament whether each new Bill complies with the European Convention. Parliamentarians will need an independent source of expert advice on the international standards, and the way in which they have been interpreted in the courts, if they are to be able to question Ministers effectively. Elected representatives in the Scottish Parliament and in the Northern Ireland and Welsh Assemblies will equally need this expert assistance.

We argued that the Commission should similarly review existing legislation and policy, within its broad responsibility to advise government and Parliament on the adequacy of the arrangements in the UK for the protection of human rights. It might be expected, in particular, to monitor the effectiveness of the Human Rights Act.

In relation to enforcement, we argued that the Commission should not, as in some jurisdictions abroad, provide an alternative complaints machinery to that of the courts. Although such a procedure would be less expensive than court proceedings, we considered it too resource intensive to be feasible at this stage. Moreover, as it is not possible to anticipate the volume nor nature of cases which will arise under the Human Rights Act, it makes sense to assess the extent to which the courts are providing effective remedies before providing an alternative system.

We did, however, see a key role for the Commission in ensuring access to justice: in providing advice and assistance to individuals who believe that their rights have been infringed. The Commission would provide legal representation for selected cases, whether for a narrow range of test cases or more broadly, depending on resources. It should also have the power to initiate its own litigation when no 'victim' was available to take a case. The absence of this power for the Northern Ireland Human Rights Commission is a major weakness. It would intervene in cases taken by others, with the leave of the court, a role frequently played by the Human Rights and Equal Opportunity Commission in Australia. In addition to advising individuals directly, we suggested that the Commission should also provide a training, information and advice service to legal advisers, ensuring that they had the expertise and access to information needed to advise on the changing standards under the Human Rights Act. We recommended ways in which the Commission might ensure that it was accessible to those sections of the public for whom communicating with a statutory body is most difficult.

The Commission should have the powers necessary to investigate alleged human rights abuses, where appropriate by conducting a public inquiry. Inquiries provide the means to address a serious incident or apparent systematic human rights abuses which cannot be resolved by litigation in the courts. They can serve to raise public awareness of the need for change and would lead to recommendations to the appropriate authority. The Northern Ireland Commission will be seriously weakened if it does not have the necessary powers to carry out such investigations.

The Commission, finally, would have a role, if limited, at the international level. It would assist the government and the UN supervisory bodies in their supervision of the UK's record in relation to UN Conventions and would be likely to assist in the establishment of national human rights institutions in countries with which the UK has a close relationship, particularly those in the Commonwealth.

In Chapter 5, covering the structure and accountability of the Commission, we considered first the implications of devolution. Recognising that the UK government will remain responsible for conformity to international human rights standards throughout the UK, we suggested that the Chief Commissioner of the Northern Ireland Human Rights Commission should be a member of the UK body.

For Britain, we concluded that an entirely London – based Commission would be unlikely to have either the public support nor the local expertise needed in Scotland and Wales. We suggested that separate Human Rights Commissioners should be appointed for Scotland, Wales and England. The Commission would be chaired by a UK Human Rights Commissioner based in London who would take responsibility for those functions of the Commission which could not be devolved to the regional level.

We suggested that it would be feasible to establish the Human Rights Commission as a separate body, working alongside those existing statutory bodies in the human rights field. The heads of those bodies could be ex officio Commissioners of the Human Rights Commission to facilitate co-ordination of their work. This approach would avoid the need to negotiate change with the existing bodies, and any re-location costs. In the long term, however, we suggested that it would prove to be neither the most effective, nor cost-effective, model.

We argued that there would be significant advantages in the long term for the Human Rights Commission to bring within its umbrella, in some form, the existing equality Commissions and the proposed Disability Rights Commission. We also suggested that the Data Protection Registrar could usefully come within the remit of the Commission and that the participation of a number of other organisations could be considered if the principle of an overarching Human Rights Commission is accepted.

In Northern Ireland, similarly, we suggested that the government should re-consider whether the proposed Equality Commission could, most effectively, work within the same structure as the Human Rights Commission. Issues investigated by that Commission, inquiries conducted, research and promotion work, will often involve discrimination issues. Discrimination cases, equally, may raise other human rights concerns - of privacy, of the right to family life or access to a fair hearing.

Within the umbrella bodies, we suggested that the heads of the existing statutory bodies should remain as named Commissioners, retaining their statutory responsibilities unless or until those responsibilities were invested in the Commission as a whole. The full UK Human Rights Commission could thus comprise: the UK Human Rights Commissioner (chair), the Scottish, Welsh and English Human Rights Commissioners, the Chief Commissioner of the Northern Ireland Human Rights Commission; the Race Equality Commissioner, Gender Equality Commissioner, Privacy Commissioner, Disability Rights Commissioner (and perhaps the Chair of the Northern Ireland Equality Commission). A Children's Rights Commissioner should, in our view, be an early addition to the Commission.

We set out the series of advantages which we foresaw in bringing the existing bodies together in this way: that it would provide a one-stop shop for individuals, employers and public bodies and enable the Commission, in turn, to deal with all aspects of a case; that it would enhance the status, public acceptability and influence of the existing single issue bodies; that it would enable savings to be made from common services; that it would enable additional Commissioners to be appointed if the government wanted to demonstrate that priority was being given to a particular issue or group (such as elderly people or children); and that, unlike single issue organisations, it would have the flexibility to shift its resources and priorities onto new issues of concern as they arose.

We also addressed the concerns that have been expressed about the umbrella model: that, by retaining named Commissioners responsible for separate areas of discrimination it would provide *insufficient* integration; that it could lead to certain issues being marginalised; that it would lead to competition for resources; that it would entail the loss of the multi-member lay Commissions; that it would involve time-consuming negotiations among the existing bodies and entail relocation costs; and answered each of those concerns in turn.

Noting that the UN's Paris Principles rightly require national human rights institutions to be able to operate independently of government, we suggested that the Commissioners should be appointed by the Crown but with the approval of Parliament, and be dismissable only by both Houses of Parliament. Within the overall budget approved by Parliament, the Commission should be able to determine the allocation of its resources.

The Commission, we argued, should have a close relationship with Parliament. It should report regularly to the proposed Parliamentary Human Rights Committee and act as its advisor. It might also be expected to advise other Select Committees on the human rights implications of the issue under investigation.

It would also be important for the work of the Commission to be transparent to the public and to those statutory and voluntary organisations most concerned with its work. We advocated statutory advisory councils be appointed by the Commission to provide a forum for dialogue with a wide range of organisations and individuals.

Finally, we noted that the UK Commission in its first year, operating as a separate body, would cost in the region of £2.8 million. We suggested that the Commission could legitimately raise additional funds from private and charitable sources for specific research, education or promotion work. It could also charge some organisations for training and advice services.

This report has thus set out the case for a Human Rights Commission for the UK, in its domestic and international context. It has also made recommendations for the structure and functions of the Northern Ireland Commission. Statutory bodies, established with adequate powers and resources, with a broad mandate and range of functions, could make a very significant contribution to the enjoyment of human rights throughout the country. They would provide the *essential* means to achieve the Government's objective: that the Human Rights Act should prevent human rights infringements by public authorities, enable individuals to enforce their rights in court and lead to a culture of rights and responsibilities. An effective Human Rights Commission would form a natural part of the Government's wider strategy to reform the way in which Britain and Northern Ireland are governed.

1. The 'Paris Principles':

Principles relating to the status of National Institutions

General Assembly Resolution 48/134 of 20 December 1993.

Competence and responsibilities

1. A national institution shall be vested with competence to promote and protect human rights.
2. A national institution shall be given as broad a mandate as possible, which shall be clearly set forth in a constitutional or legislative text, specifying its constitution and its sphere of competence.
3. A national institution shall, *inter alia*, have the following responsibilities:

(a) To submit to the Government, Parliament and any other competent body, on an advisory basis either at the request of the authorities concerned or through the exercise of its power to hear a matter without higher referral, opinions, recommendations, proposals and reports on any matters concerning the promotion and protection of human rights; the national institution may decide to publicise them; these opinions, recommendations, proposals and reports, as well as any prerogative of the national institution, shall relate to the following areas:

(i) Any legislative or administrative provisions, as well as provisions relating to judicial organisation, intended to preserve and extend the protection of human rights; in that connection, the national institution shall examine the legislation and administrative provisions in force, as well as bills and proposals, and shall make such recommendations as it deems appropriate in order to ensure that these provisions conform to the fundamental principles of human rights; it shall, if necessary, recommend the adoption of new legislation, the amendment of legislation in force and the adoption or amendment of administrative measures;

(ii)   Any situation of violation of human rights which it decides to take up;

(iii)   The preparation of reports on the national situation with regard to human rights in general, and on more specific matters;

(iv)   Drawing the attention of the Government to situations in any part of the country where human rights are violated and making proposals to it for initiatives to put an end to such situations and, where necessary, expressing an opinion on the positions and reactions of the Government;

(b) To promote and ensure the harmonisation of national legislation, regulations and practices with the international human rights instruments to which the State is a party, and their effective implementation;

(c) To encourage ratification of the above-mentioned instruments or accession to those instruments, and to ensure their implementation;

(d) To contribute to the reports which States are required to submit to United Nations bodies and committees, and to regional institutions, pursuant to their treaty obligations, and, where necessary, to express an opinion on the subject, with due respect for their independence;

(e) To co-operate with the United Nations and the United Nations system, the regional institutions and the national institutions of other countries that are competent in the areas of the promotion and protection of human rights;

(f) To assist in the formulation of programmes for the teaching of and research into human rights and to take part in their execution in schools, universities and professional circles;

(g) To publicise human rights and efforts to combat all forms of discrimination, in particular racial discrimination, by increasing public awareness; especially through information and education and by making use of all press organs.

Composition and guarantees of independence and pluralism

1. The composition of the national institution and the appointment of its members, whether by means of an election or otherwise,

shall be established in accordance with a procedure which affords all necessary guarantees to ensure the pluralist representation of the social forces (of civilian society) involved in the promotion and protection of human rights, particularly by powers which will enable effective co-operation to be established with, or through the presence of, representatives of:

(a) Non-governmental organisations responsible for human rights and efforts to combat racial discrimination, trade unions, concerned social and professional organisations, for example, associations of lawyers, doctors, journalists and eminent scientists;

(b) Trends in philosophical or religious thought;

(c) Universities and qualified experts;

(d) Parliament;

(e) Government departments (if they are included, these representatives should participate in the deliberations only in an advisory capacity).

2. The national institution shall have an infrastructure which is suited to the smooth conduct of its activities, in particular adequate funding. The purpose of this funding should be to enable it to have its own staff and premises, in order to be independent of the Government and not to be subject to financial control which might affect its independence.

3. In order to ensure a stable mandate for the members of the institution, without which there can be no real independence, their appointment shall be affected by an official act which shall establish the specific duration of the mandate. This mandate may be renewable, provided that the pluralism of the institution's membership is ensured.

Methods of operation

Within the framework of its operation, the national institution shall:

(a) Freely consider any questions falling within its competence, whether they are submitted by the Government or taken up by it without referral to a higher authority, on the proposal of its members or of any petitioner;

(b) Hear any person and obtain any information and any documents necessary for assessing situations falling within its competence;

(c) Address public opinion directly or through any press organ, particularly in order to publicise its opinions and recommendations;

(d) Meet on a regular basis and whenever necessary in the presence of all of its members after they have been duly convened;

(e) Establish working groups from among its members as necessary, and set up local or regional sections to assist it in discharging its functions;

(f) Maintain consultation with other bodies, whether jurisdictional or otherwise, responsible for the promotion and protection of human rights (in particular, ombudsmen, mediators and similar institutions);

(g) In view of the fundamental role played by non-governmental organisations in expanding the work of national institutions, develop relations with non-governmental organisations devoted to promoting and protecting human rights, to economic and social development, to combating racism, to protecting particularly vulnerable groups, (especially children, migrant workers, refugees, physically and mentally disabled persons) or to specialised areas.

Additional principles concerning the status of commissions with quasi-jurisdictional competence

A national institution may be authorised to hear and consider complaints and petitions concerning individual situations. Cases may be brought before it by individuals, their representatives, third parties, non-governmental organisations, associations of trade unions or other representative organisations. In such circumstances, and without prejudice to the principles stated above concerning the other powers of the commissions, the functions entrusted to them may be based on the following principles:

(a) Seeking an amicable settlement through conciliation or, within the limits prescribed by the law, through binding decisions or, where necessary, on the basis of confidentiality;

(b) Informing the party who filed the petition of his rights, in particular the remedies available to him, and promoting his access to them;

(c) Hearing any complaints or petitions or transmitting them to any other competent authority within the limits prescribed by the law;

(d) Making recommendations to the competent authorities, especially by proposing amendments or reforms of the laws, regulations and administrative practices, especially if they have created the difficulties encountered by the persons filing the petitions in order to assert their rights.

Appendix 2: Council of Europe Recommendations on national human rights institutions

Recommendation No.R (97) 14 of the Committee of Ministers to Member States on the Establishment of Independent National Human Rights Institutions

Adopted by the Committee of Ministers on 30 September 1997 at the 602nd meeting of the Ministers' Deputies

The Committee of Ministers, under the terms of Article 15.b of the Statute of the Council of Europe,

Whereas the aim of the Council of Europe is to achieve a greater unity between its members, in particular through the maintenance and further realisation of human rights and fundamental freedoms;

Taking into account Resolution 48/134 on national institutions for the promotion and protection of human rights adopted by the General Assembly of the United Nations on 20 December 1993 as well as relevant resolutions adopted by the Commission on Human Rights of the United Nations;

Taking into account also the Vienna Declaration and Programme of Action adopted by the World Conference on Human Rights on 25 June 1993;

Recalling its Recommendation No. R (85) 13 on the institution of the *ombudsman*, adopted on 23 September 1985;

Recalling the terms of Resolution No. 2 adopted at the 1st European Meeting of the National Institutions for the Promotion and Protection of Human Rights, held in Strasbourg from 7 to 9 November 1994 under the auspices of the Council of Europe, and the declaration adopted at the second such meeting, held in Copenhagen from 22 to 22 January 1997;

Considering that the maintenance and further realization of human rights, as safeguarded by both national legislation and international instruments, are conditional upon a more thorough knowledge and widespread awareness of human rights issues;

Convinced that the fulfilment of these conditions, which are essential for the reinforcement and promotion of democracy, could profitably be entrusted to independent institutions established according to law for the promotion and protection of human rights (hereinafter referred to as 'national human rights institutions'), to be responsible for, *inter alia*, drawing the public authorities' attention too, and advising them on, human rights matters and promoting the provision of human rights information and education for the public;

Welcoming the fact that national human rights institutions have been established in several member States;

Convinced, in the light of experience, that it is desirable to promote the establishment of national human rights institutions in the member States where comparable institutions do not exist,

Recommends that the governments of member States:

a.   consider, taking account of the specific requirements of each member State, the possibility of establishing effective national human rights institutions, in particular human rights commissions which are pluralist in their membership, ombudsmen or comparable institutions;

b.   draw, as appropriate, on the experience acquired by existing national human rights commissions and other national human rights institutions, having regard to the principles set out in Resolution 48/134 of the General Assembly of the United Nations and in the Vienna Declaration and Programme of Action, adopted in 1993, as well as on the experience acquired by ombudsmen, having regard to Recommendation No.R (85) 13 of the Committee of Ministers;

c.   promote cooperation, in particular through exchange of information and experience, between national human rights institutions and between them and the Council of Europe, in accordance with Resolution (97) 11 of the Committee of Ministers;

d.   ensure that this recommendation is distributed in civil society, in particular among non-governmental organisations.

Resolution (97) 11 on Co-operation between National Human Rights Institutions of Member States and between them and the Council of Europe

Adopted by the Committee of Ministers on 30 September 1997, at the 602nd meeting of the Ministers' Deputies

The Committee of Ministers, under the terms of Article 15.a of the Statute of the Council of Europe,

Considering that the maintenance and further realisation of human rights and fundamental freedoms is one of the principal tasks assigned to the Council of Europe under its Statute;

Recalling its Recommendation No. R (97) 14 on the establishment of independent national human rights institutions;

Having regard to the importance of the role of such institutions, in particular in providing information about human rights to both the public authorities and civil society;

Aware that the provision of information on this subject does much to safeguard and promote human rights and fundamental freedoms, provided the information is comprehensive, up to date and wide-ranging;

Considering that it is therefore of the utmost importance that the national human rights institutions established in member states have access to sources of information about human rights;

Bearing in mind the desirability of improved information of the national human rights institutions on each other's activities as well as those of the Council of Europe in the field of human rights;

Convinced that the organisation of regular meetings with these institutions, with the participation of Council of Europe bodies dealing with human rights, would be an effective means of promoting human rights,

Decides:

a. to institute, in the framework of the Council of Europe, regular meetings with national human rights institutions of member states to exchange views and experience on the promotion and protection of human rights in their areas of competence:

b. to instruct the Secretary General to invite Council of Europe bodies dealing with human rights to attend such meetings with a view to facilitating exchanges of views and experience on questions of mutual interest;

c. to invite the Secretary General to ensure that national human rights institutions are informed of relevant activities concerning the promotion and protection of human rights in the framework of the Council of Europe.

3. Proposed UK Human Rights Commission: costing of first year[1]

Timing considerations

1   The task is to estimate the cost of setting up and operating a new Human Rights Commission 'in its first year'. For estimating purposes, we need to identify which financial year should be taken as 'the first year'. This also means making assumptions about the length of time it would take, following enactment of the legislation, for the HRC to be in a position to begin its operations and about how costs are to be allocated within financial years.

2   If we assume Royal Assent to the legislation in the Summer of 1998, it would be unlikely that key preliminary tasks - like the identification and recruitment of key personnel and the hiring of premises and structural conversion - would have been completed much before the turn of the year. Even then, there would still remain the recruitment of the rest of the staff, the procurement and installation of equipment, basic training and the introduction of the appropriate financial and administrative systems. It may not even be clear until near the end of the PES 98 process (Public Expenditure Survey) in October/November precisely what the HRC would have to spend in 1999-2000. It would be sensible, in the light of this, to assume that the HRC would be in a position to open its doors for business not much before end March 1999.

3   This does not mean, of course, that everything would stand still until then. One would expect the Commissioner and the Executive director, once appointed, to have developed some operational plans in the meantime and the Commission itself to have met and engaged in some strategic thinking. This advance work would be progressively strengthened as more staff came on stream and this would ensure that the new organisation would not start entirely from cold on 1st April 1999; but, before then, it seems unlikely to be in a position to do much to put its ideas into effect.

4   In accounting terms, this suggests that the first full operational year should be regarded as 1999-2000. The costings have been prepared on this basis. For the purposes of PES 97, there would

have to be assumptions about the amount of expenditure - mostly start-up costs - likely to fall in the latter half of 1998-99. There are also references in this document to the resource implications for year 2; by which is meant the financial year 2000-01.

Functions and levels of activity

5   The main functions of the HRC fall conveniently into four operating sections under the Executive Director and form the natural building blocks for costing the organisation. These are: the Legal Section, the Policy Section, the Press and Promotion Section and the Support Services Section. The detailed costings below are based on this structure with the addition of some specific activities that do not fall naturally within the main operating sections.

6   Some realistic assumptions would have to be made about the levels of activity under the various functional headings in year one and about speed of take off. This means also making assumptions about the political environment and, in particular, about the Commission's own priorities. These assumptions, and the suggested conclusions on the resources needed to carry them into effect, are set out below. The conclusions on staff costs are derived from the average staff costs in this financial year of relevant grades in a government department (in this case, the Home Office). This seems appropriate as it is very likely that most of the HRC staff would be employed on analogous Civil Service terms and conditions of service and would form part of the Civil Service Superannuation scheme. These unit costs are set out in Table 1. It should be noted that the estimates are based on current costs. It is no longer good government practice to attempt to take account of future wage inflation.

Legal section - the selective scrutiny of legislation, advice on test cases and individual queries and on human rights issues generally.

7   The HRC would go live in the middle of a new Labour Government's second Parliamentary session. This could coincide with constitutional legislation with a considerable bearing on

human rights issues. In a normal Parliamentary session, major departments could expect to have (say) two major programme Bills, but by no means all departments would be legislating in areas with a human rights interest. What would be needed is a capacity for screening legislative proposals (primary and secondary) for a prima facie indication of a human rights interest followed by a selection of proposals for a more intensive examination. A crude assumption for year 1 might be that some four main programme Bills would need closer scrutiny and (say) six major SI or Orders in Council. I doubt whether it is feasible to make an estimate of relevant EU legislation - bearing in mind that many areas of human rights sensitivity for the moment lie outside EU competence. That said, there might well be proposals arising out of agreements under the Third Pillar which required administrative or legislative action by government and which might have human rights implications- for example in the field of immigration. It is impossible to quantify this potential work at this stage. This needs to be noted as a work area which might well expand, particularly in year 2, and whose staffing implications would have to be assessed in the light of experience.

8   It is difficult to envisage a significant test case programme in the first year. A careful strategy would need to be built up, and even if a suitable case were identified, the amount of preparatory work that would be needed suggests that it is unlikely to have got beyond the stage of Counsel's Opinion by the end of the year. We cannot be sure, however, that the HRC in its first year would not want to take advantage of incorporation and make its mark early on, so it would be prudent to allow for some such work. A lot of this would have to be done in-house, but there should be opportunities for contracting out. This, however, would depend on the nature of the case and on the other pressures on the in-house team.

9   Aside from these primary matters, it has to be assumed that there would be an on-going demand for legal advice on human rights matters generally, particularly from the Policy and investigation sections. There would also be the normal run of organisational

legal matters (for example, on property) and on matters to do with the HRC's own statutory powers. There would be obvious scope for farming out the former.

10   For the work described above, therefore, the Legal Section would be substantially loaded with good quality work demanding a specialist expertise. A conservative estimate of the staffing requirement would be 1 Head of Section (Grade 5 equivalent) with 1 PS (personal secretary), 3 Assistant Lawyers (Grade 7 equivalent) and 1 Junior Lawyer (SEO) with 1 PS and 2 Administrative Assistants (AO equivalent). There would also need to be a budget for externally contracted legal work, including any test case preparation. It would be prudent to make a generous contingency provision for this - say £400K.

11   There would also be legal work coming under this section arising out of the advice function for individual enquirers. This function enters unknown territory and attempts at too much precision would be spurious. One starting point would be to assume a level of interest at least equivalent to the total number of requests received by the CRE each year for assistance - which currently total some 10,000 before they are reduced to the level at which formal assistance procedures are engaged. This, of course, represents the level of activity of a mature, well established and high profile body with extensive enforcement powers. For the HRC in year 1, it would seem defensible to scale down the likely estimate of activity to the order of 7,000 enquiries. It is assumed that the response to individual enquiries would not be resource intensive, that is to say that they would be restricted to written or telephone replies and confined to explaining the avenues of redress available under existing law with details of whom to contact in order to pursue the matter further. Some enquiries would be capable of being answered on the spot; others would need some research. In the most difficult cases, a legal view might be needed. If we assume that 10 per cent of the estimated enquiries fall in this category, then lawyers in the Legal Section might have to cope with 500 such cases. It has to be assumed that the complement proposed above would be sufficient for this.

12   For working purposes, I assume a 50-50 split between the cases requiring further research and those which could be disposed of on the telephone. At that level of activity (about 630 cases a month) and allowing for 2 hours in a difficult case and no more than 15 minutes in a straightforward one, it is hard to see a case for more than 3 staff (1 SEO, 1 HEO and 1 EO equivalent) with access to a typist. The staff need not be legally qualified although thorough training would be required - for which a dedicated provision - say £20K - should be made. But it should be noted that this function would be very vulnerable to short term or unexpected pressures and it would not be surprising, in those events, for this to be revealed as an underestimate.

13   IPPR proposes that this section provide service providers with advice on good practice. I have not at this stage made separate provision for this as I foresee some time elapsing before the HRC has worked up the sort of detailed codes of practice to which it could put its name in specific areas and cast them in a form suitable for public use.

14   It has to be said of this as well as of other sections of the HRC that the scope for expansion of work in year 2 is considerable - particularly in respect of the demand driven enquiry work where it would not be surprising to see a volume of work necessitating a doubling of the present very modest proposals for this small sub-section. A strategic decision by the Commission to concentrate on the vetting of legislation and test case work, which is not impossible against the background of new legislation of this nature, would also have significant manpower implications.

Policy section

15   This section would have three sub-sections: formal inquiries and investigations; research; and policy coordination. It would need to be headed by a senior staff member. He or she should have appropriate human rights experience or background. The intellectual content of the work and the potential management content with expansion beyond year 1 justifies a Grade 5 equivalent (with PS).

Inquiries/investigations

16   In year 1 this sub-section would need to give priority to working up a general approach and strategy on the selection of subjects for formal inquiries and on methods of operation. Developmental work would be needed on the market for training courses directed at external organisations. In terms of results on the ground, it is difficult to see much more than the start of one (or two at the most) inquiries and these may well not have been finished by the end of the first year. It is assumed that the maximum use would be made in such inquiries of external Commissioners for whom fees would be necessary.

17   The post of head of the sub-section does not necessarily call for a qualified lawyer - although some legal experience might well prove helpful. It would be graded at the equivalent level of Grade 7. There would need to be support on the policy and training fronts with administrative and secretarial help in addition. All of this would require, in addition to the Head of Section, 2 staff (one a training specialist) at HEO equivalent, 1 administrative assistant at AO equivalent and 1 PS. In year 2, it is almost certain that there would be more formal inquiries and that this level of support staff would need to increase.

18   There would also need to be a budget for fees for external Commissioners. Given the specialised legal background likely to be required, a contingency assumption (hopefully too generous) of £500 a day might be prudent. If the inquiry work required 20 Commissioner days, that would make for a allocation of £10K to which £5K should be added for travel, hearings, hire of rooms etc:- making a total of £15K.

Research

19   The main activity on this front in year 1 would be acquiring books and periodicals, linking into the academic research network, preparing a literature survey and drawing up a research strategy for the Commission. It is possible, but not certain, that some specific research might be commissioned towards the end of the year. At this very early stage I would not see a need for more than 1

Research Officer but, given the level at which he or she would be dealing in the academic world this should be pitched at a suuitably senior equivalent rank-specifically Grade 7 with 1 Research Assistant

(HEO equivalent). There would also need to be a budget for library and periodical acquisitions (say £5K) and for preliminary commissioning costs for any external research project (say £50K) making £55K in total. For year 2, it is likely that there would be scope for more commissioned and in-house research and the staffing would need to reflect this. It might also be possible in year 2 to attract charitable funding for research purposes.

Policy co-ordination

20   As already suggested, the functions of this sub section would cover:

- Development and coordination of corporate policy as regards the HRC as finally constituted and on human rights areas not covered by existing bodies.
- Servicing of Commission and Advisory Council.
- The consultative process on the incorporation of existing bodies.
- Production of Annual Report.

22   The staffing requirements of this sub-section are estimated at : 1 Head of sub-section (Grade 7 equivalent), 1 PS, 3 Policy Assistants (2 HEO/AT and 1 EO equivalents) and 1 Administrative Assistant (AO). There will need to be adequate provision for travelling or meetings in connection with the consultation exercise - say 10K. In year 2, a process of assimilating certain policy functions presently covered by existing bodies would have staffing implications.

Press and promotion section

23   The HRC would undoubtedly want to make an event of its launch and to follow it up in year 1 with events, publications and seminars to draw attention to the incorporation legislation and its implications and to the work of the HRC itself - even if it had to do so at a time when its policies were still evolving. There would also be an on going, unprompted press interest. (I have not assumed for

year 1 that this section would be able to produce material for sale - for example, to schools. But this is an activity which, for year 2, could be an income generator in its own right and which might attract charitable funding. Some staff strengthening would be necessary, however, for this purpose). On this basis, staff requirements would include 1 Head of Section (SEO salary equivalent) with 1 Press Officer (HEO equivalent), 1 Promotions Officer (HEO), for publications and events and 1 Promotions Officer (HEO) for general promotion work, including Parliamentary liaison. An events budget might amount to £30K and the publications budget to £100K with (say) £20K for a Parliamentary consultancy service.

Support services section

24   This section would be responsible for: financial control; office services, including IT and procurement; personnel matters; and training. As with all new NDPBs, the National Audit Office could be expected to take a close interest in the financial control systems in particular. It would be unwise to skimp on the quality of staff in this area. The staff structure would be likely to be as follows: 1 Head of Section (Grade 6 equivalent) with 1 PS, 1 Financial Controller (SEO) with 1 Financial Assistant (EO), 1 Office Manager (SEO) with 1 Assistant/IT manager (EO), 1 Personnel and Training Manager (SEO) with 1 Personnel Assistant (EO) and 1 Training Assistant (EO). There should be administrative support in the shape of 1 AO, and I suggest making provision for 2 typists to serve the section as a whole. A staff training budget should be provided at (say) £50K.

25   It may be argued that the size of this section would be disproportionate to the size of the organisation as a whole. Given the public sector context, however, it is important to get the operation under way with an adequate support infrastructure. If the operational side of the Commission expanded in the near future, the relative size of this section would quickly diminish.

Other running costs

Chair and Executive Director

26   It is assumed that there would be a full time Chair - the UK Human Rights Commissioner - as well as an Executive Director. Salaries would probably have to be determined personally on a recruitment and retention basis - and the Treasury might demand a say in the process. It would be prudent to budget on the basis of a Grade 3 salary for the Chair and a Grade 5 plus salary for the Executive Director. There would need to be 2 PS to support this senior management function.

International representation

27   There would be likely to be very few international conferences of significance to attend in the course of any one year but it would be important that the HRC be represented at them. There might also be introductory or familiarisation visits - for example, to the Human Rights Directorate in Strasbourg. Assuming that these initial visits were confined to Europe in year 1, a budget of £5K should cover travel and subsistence for two. An additional allowance of £10K should cover peregrinations further afield.

Standard office on-costs

28.   Assumptions would have to be made about the standard items of on-costs. The most significant item of these would be in respect of rent and rates. A reasonably approximate figure for this can be derived from a standard figure (£50) for square footage in inner London, an assumption of approx 6,000 square feet for an office of 40 staff with conference and storage facilities and a comparison with the expenditure of other NDPBs on the same item adjusted for the relative sizes. On this basis, provision for rent and rates, would be about £320K (premises) and £30K (rates). It would be desirable, however, to add to this by a sum large enough to act as a contingency or to allow for expansion. On this reasoning, it would be prudent to allow for a provision of £400K. Of the remaining items, the estimates can be derived from comparisons with other bodies. Taking all this into account, the projections of on-costs in thousands are as follows:

On – Costs

	in £000s
Rent and rates	400
Maintenance, cleaning, heating and lighting	50
Office supplies, printing and stationery	20
Postage and telephone	50
Travel and subsistence	15
Audit fee	6
IT Service contract	8
TOTAL (say) £550	

Staff

29   The total cost of the staff numbers (40 in all) identified above - including the Chair's salary costs - is **£1.5 million** The staff structure by analagous Civil Service salary grade is in Table 2.

Budgets allocated to specific functions (see above).

30. These can be summarised as follows:

	£000s
Legal	400
Training (enquiry staff)	20
Commissioners' fees	15
Research	55
Printing	100 (say)
International	15
Consultation	10
Staff training (general)	50
Parliamentary consultancy	20
Events	30
TOTAL	**745**

Total first full year costs.

31   **The total estimated cost for the HRC's first full year 1999-2000 is therefore £2.8 million**

Costs in period July 1998 - April 1999.

32   The one-off start-up costs would be expected to fall in this period together with some staff and other running costs. The start-up costs are estimated as follows:

	£ 000s
IT installation @ £1400 per 46 Pcs	64.4
2 Fax machines @ £1000 each	2
15 printers @ £300 per printer	4.5
Databases	10
Carpeting and decorations	25
Furniture	23
Telephones	10
Lighting adjustments	3
TOTAL	**(say) 142**

33   Some running costs would fall in this period. It is pointless at this distance to forecast the pace of recruitment and the consequential incidence of on-costs. As a crude measure we might assume expenditure equivalent to one quarter's expenditure on staff and on-costs. On this basis, running costs for 1998/9 would total £512K. This makes for a total expenditure (setting-up and running) for this year of £654K.

Conclusion

34   Two things need to be emphasised. The first is that, although there are plenty of precedents for the funding of NDPBs, this one would be entering substantially new and, potentially at least, politically controversial territory. Opinions would differ, quite legitimately, on priorities and strategies. The assumptions on levels of activity have therefore had to be bold. The second point is that, as has been constantly reiterated in the body of this paper, the potential for growth in year 2 is very considerable. This paper has not attempted detailed estimates for year 2, if only because the degree of sheer speculation would have vitiated the exercise and because it would also involve political assumptions about the availability of funding which it is not possible to make. But one thing is clear. The expectations of the new body will be very great. It is this factor that should most influence PES estimates for that year.

Table 1
Average staff costs by Civil Service grade
1997/98   **£**

Chief Inspector/Grade 4	80,414
Grade 5	65,613
Supt. Inspector (Scientific)	69,793
Grade 6	63,284
Grade 7	44,454
SEO	34,618
HEO (D)	29,654
HEO	28,547
AT	23,110
EO	23,060
AO	16,655
AA	14,242
SPS	26,486
Ps	22,473
Typist	19,044

Table: 2
Staff structure and costings of HRC
Civil Service

Equivalent Grade	numbers	Cost (£000s)
3	1	80
5+	1	70
5	2	132
6	1	63.2
7	6	267
SEO	6	207.6
HEO	9	256.5
EO	8	184
AO	5	83.5

Endnote

[1] Estimate drawn up by Michael Head in April 1997

4. Respondents to IPPR Consultation Papers

Organisations and individuals who responded to IPPR's Consultation Paper *A UK Human Rights Commission : the Options* published in December 1996 or to the subsequent paper circulated in May 1997. Many others responded in meetings organised to discuss the proposals.

The Commission for Racial Equality (GB)
The Equal Opportunities Commission (GB)
The Equal Opportunities Commission (Northern Ireland)
The Standing Advisory Commission on Human Rights (NI)
The Data Protection Registrar
The Law Society
Professor Tom Hadden
Professor Brice Dickson (Committee on the Administration of Justice, Belfast)
The Children's Rights Office
The Royal College of Nursing
Professor Colm Campbell
Professor Alan Miller (Scottish Council for Civil Liberties)
The Immigration Law Practitioners Association
The Runnymede Trust
Professor Bhikhu Parekh
Francesca Klug
Director of Liberty (National Council for Civil Liberties)
Professor Nicola Lacey
Children in Scotland
The Royal National Institute for Deaf People
Sally Stepanian
Charter 87
The Minority Rights Group
Ann Dummett
Rabinder Singh
Disability Awareness in Action
Ben Whitaker
Robin Wilson (Democratic Dialogue)
Article 19

The Refugee Council
The Churches Commission for Racial Justice
Michael Nicholls
The Discrimination Law Association
Amnesty Lawyers Group
Association of Charitable Foundations
British Irish Rights Watch
Françoise Hampson
Professor Michael Banton
1990 Trust

5. Agendas for IPPR Conferences
Consultative conference on the *Options for a UK Human Rights Commission,* 18 December 1996.

9.45   Chair's introduction: **Françoise Hampson**

10.00   **Jack Straw MP**, Shadow Home Secretary

10.45   Coffee

11.15   *The international experience*

      Brian Burdekin, Special Advisor to the UN High Commissioner on Human Rights; former Australian Human Rights Commissioner

12.00   *UK Human Rights Commission: the options*

      Sarah Spencer, Director, IPPR Human Rights Programme

      Ian Bynoe, IPPR Research Fellow

1.00   Lunch

2.15   *Relationship with the existing official human rights bodies*

      Joan Smyth, Chair and Chief Executive, Northern Ireland Equal Opportunities Commission

      Herman Ouseley, Chairman, Commission for Racial Equality

      Bob Cooper, Chairman, Fair Employment Commission

      Elizabeth France, Data Protection Registrar

3.45   Tea

4.15   *NGO perspective on the options*

      Brice Dickson, Committee on the Administration of Justice, Northern Ireland

      Alan Miller, Scottish Council for Civil Liberties

      John Wadham, Liberty

      Discussion

5.00   Conclusion: **Françoise Hampson**

IPPR/CHRI Conference: *Commonwealth Human Rights Institutions – Promoting Good Practice* **16-17 October 1997.**

9.00   Registration

9.30   **Welcome**
Chair: **Shirley Mabusela**, Deputy Chairperson, South African Human Rights Commission

Keynote Addresses
Chief Emeka Anyaoku – Commonwealth Secretary – General
Tony Lloyd MP – Minister of State, UK Foreign and Commonwealth Office
Dr Kamal Hossain – Former Minister of Law and Minister of Foreign Affairs, Bangladesh and Chair, Advisory Commission to the Commonwealth Human Rights Initiative

11.00   **Coffee**

11.30   *The importance of national human rights institutions – the UN and Commonwealth perspectives*
Brian Burdekin – Special Advisor to the UN High Commissioner for Human Rights; former Australian Human Rights Commissioner.

Co-ordinating human rights institutions – The African perspective
Dr Solomon Gwei – Chairman, Cameroon National Human Rights Commission; Co-ordinator, African national human rights institutions
Discussion

13.00   **Lunch**

14.00   *Operational challenges [funding, independence from Government, handling of complaints, prioritising resources, media relations]*
Margaret Sekaggya – Chairperson, National Human Rights Commission, Uganda

Dr Maria Alice Mabota – President, Liga Moçambicana Dos Direitos Humanos

Michael Auret – National Director, Catholic Commission for Justice and Peace, Zimbabwe

15.30   Tea

16.00   **Workshops:**

a How to get a national human rights institution established

Brian Burdekin – Special Adviser to the UN High Commissioner for Human Rights

b Accessibility/Enforcement/complaints function

Livingstone Sewanyana – Executive Director, Foundation for Human Rights Initiative, Uganda

c Relationship to Parliament/Government/public bodies
Pamela Jefferies – Chief Commissioner, New Zealand Human Rights Commission

d Use of media and public affairs in human rights education and promotion

Margie Cook – Manager, Public Affairs, Australian Human Rights and Equal Opportunity Commission

17.30   Close

17 October 1997

9.30   *Unlawful detention, torture and degrading treatment*
Emile Short – Chairman and Administrative Head, Commission on Human Rights and Administrative Justice, Ghana

Refugees
Nick Hardwick – Director, Refugee Council, United Kingdom

10.45   Coffee

11.15   *Children's Rights*
Shri RV Pillai, Secretary General, Indian Human Rights Commission

Women's Rights
Maja Daruwala – Director, Commonwealth Human Rights Initiative, New Delhi
Socio-economic rights
Shirley Mabusela – Deputy Chairperson, South African Human Rights Commission
Julia Haüserman – President, Rights and Humanity

13.00   Lunch
14.00   *Discrimination Issues*
Canada: recent developments and key issues
John Hucker – Secretary General, Canadian Human Rights Commission
Religious and political discrimination
Bob Cooper – Chairman, Northern Ireland Fair Employment Commission
Alternative dispute resolution in the area of employment including disability
Pamela Jefferies – Chief Commissioner, New Zealand Human Rights Commisson

15.45   Tea
16.15   *The way forward and possibility of an umbrella body for national human rights institutions in Commonwealth countries*
Chair: **Sarah Spencer**
Panel
    Shirley Mabusela – South Africa
    Pamela Jefferies – New Zealand
    Shri RV Pillai – India
    John Hucker – Canada
    Christine Mulindwa-Matovu – Legal & Constitutional Affairs Division, Commonwealth Secretariat

17.30   Chair: Closing remarks

(MILE END)
QMW LIBRARY

WITHDRAWN
FROM STOCK
QMUL LIBRARY